Rivers untangled

This is a work of fiction and non-fiction. In the fictionalized stories of different women, all the names, characters, places, events, and incidents are either the product of the author's imagination or are used in a fictitious manner. Any resemblance to actual persons, living or dead, or actual events is coincidental. The non-fiction parts pertain to events in the author's life. The content presented therein is based on the author's creative interpretation of her perspective on lived experiences.

Photographs: Sara Angelini

First edition 2026

ISBN: 978-1-0369-6900-4 (print)

Printed in the UK

This book is offered to the reader as a conversation. As a Psychotherapist I listen to stories and facilitate conversations. Therapy is an activity that restores peace because of those conversations. It also restores balance because stories are told and heard. If we had more conversations in our everyday, with our loved ones and friends, at school and at work, and if we told each other more stories, of our pain and defeats and recognized that this is part of life, there would be more peace and balance in the world. It is not only the act of telling but the act of receiving that brings harmony. Listening with an open mind and the whole body without the need to interrupt, assume or offer solutions is an act of love. If this were an ordinary thing we did for each other, we would have more space to create and express ourselves with freedom. This is the spirit with which this book has come about.

Contents

Part I

Part II

Part I

***The river** is lying in wait. The top of the orchard is soggy, saturated heavy with water. The women decide to dig a trench alongside the path. Girls! Close your eyes and sit quietly next to the trench and you will hear the water move. Listen, as it gathers pace, rushing and gurgling. See how the water appears out of nowhere, how it gathers momentum. Even though this river is small, watch how potent she becomes, once she is set free. Capable of carrying limitless quantities of water, she journeys, like all rivers, from the land to the sea. The clouds, fed by her, release rain that feeds her sister rivers further down the valleys. The water branches out to create new streams, swirling around trees and creating islands. She goes where she needs to go. Untangled. Untamed. Flowing to lower planes, she slows down, now gently meandering, spreading her arms, and meeting the generosity of the valley. Here the land is fertile. Here people settle and grow food. Watch girls, how mama bear drags the big fat salmon under the fir tree for the family to feast on. The carcass, a potent fertilizer, feeds the trees nearby. The river, an unbridled power, forgotten or remembered, is tied to life. She is the golden liquid of the soul that carves stories into the landscape. Remember girls, setting her free and crossing her body delivers you to the beyond.*

1

April
River

April woke up with a rage in her belly.

Kenji had left the house at dawn in a rush to catch a train to Amsterdam, a regular destination for his business. *I am going to be on my own for exactly seven days*, April thought. *The girls and I will settle into a routine that is comfortable enough. And as ever, loneliness will be knocking on my door.*

April's relationship with rage was complicated. In part it was tied to her mother, whose denial of grief and anger occasionally spilt out with absurd declarations. Following April's brother's tragic death her mother hurled her sorrow at April, saying that she'd rather have her dead than him. Words no apology could take back.

As a therapist, April was sensitized to rage's younger sibling, anger, herself feeling it keenly in relation to the state of the world and the oppressive nature of misogyny. Many of her female clients struggled to feel anger. Blame was showing up more comfortably, which was never far from self-blame that had a habit of sneaking its way into the dark pit of shame. Anger and its cousins were unwelcome guests.

Today she was tired with the consuming nature of this emotion, noting that it was once more directed towards Kenji and his absences, an easy enough target. April wasn't just tired of her raging anger, but tired of Kenji's frequent business trips.

By the time April was standing in the kitchen she marked out the week on their calendar, taking note that today was day seven of the seventh month. With Kenji gone for seven days, April let that numerical constellation linger in her mind. The noise of Sora and Aya thundering down the stairs interrupted her thoughts. Who gets to the kitchen first, a daily contest. *They almost always go quiet once they sit down to eat*, April thought with a smile. They have always been hungry kids. She gave them a squeeze each, and Aya nuzzled her face into her soft belly.

Aya and Sora, whose names put together meant Beautiful Sky in Japanese, a nod to Kenji's heritage, were their identical twin daughters. *One for each*, sometimes April thought. Conceived during the cherry blossom season, when April and Kenji were hiking on Mount Fuji, there was an auspicious moment when April cupped a cluster of the delicate white and pink flowers, inhaling their scent, and catching a glimpse of the blue sky.

April watched her daughters busying themselves at the breakfast table. She heard a click in her mind, like the shutters of a camera framing them in a still life; Sora with her a habit of perching her head slightly to the right, as if listening into the beyond. Aya's hands always busy, as if searching for something, her energy a palpable drive. A loud thud brought April back. Aya had knocked the jam off the table, which reminded April of what lay ahead.

"Aya, Sora!" April said, "I realised that today is the seventh day of the seventh month and you two are in your seventh year". "And seven is your favourite number Momo" Aya shouted out. "And daddy is gone for seven days", Sora chipped in, nonchalantly. "Yes, that's interesting" April said slowly. Aya nodded keenly, while Sora went back to studying the cereal box. *More than lonely,* April thought, *I am going to feel frustrated, which is about my boredom, sitting on me like a lid!*

Realizing this made April feel better and made her want to play. She turned to the Aya and Sora and said "Right girls, for the next seven days how about you collect seven items each, one item for every day. It can be something you find outside, or something that is special to you from home. Anything really that catches your eye. Store them safely, and when daddy comes back, we do the grand reveal, like an exhibition. Yes?" "Yes!" The girls yelled, catching fire immediately as they bustled off excitedly to make plans.

April felt satisfied that she had cast the door open to the creative field of possibilities.

Once she had dropped the girls to school, she sat down at her desk by the window, her favourite place in the house. Looking out had always held promise. She sat, simply looking for a while. She noticed how the light hit the brick wall of their neighbour's house, bringing out the different shades of coral. Skinny buttercups were sprouting in the uncut grass, their shiny heads swaying in the morning breeze.

Just yesterday one of her patients had told her how terrifying it was for them to walk in uncut grass, describing how their whole body vibrated with a creepy sensation, gripping their heart and squeezing their airways. "Fucking terrifying!" they shouted as their whole body scrunched up in disgust. April smiled. She loved their unbridled swearing at all things clawing at them, a cathartic antidote to their terror. What was expansion for one, was constriction for another.

April opened her laptop. As was her habit, she opened three windows, one for her current favourite artist, still Paul Klee, one with Google maps, she typed in Amsterdam despite herself, and then one window for research, where she typed 'meaning of number seven'.

The image and description that caught her attention was the seed of life. It was a symbol that consisted of seven equally sized circles pushed together and partially superimposed creating a perfect geometrical flower. Apart from it being an ancient symbol, found across the world and in different religions, it made April think of the fertilized human cell.

April had always marvelled at the unfathomable nature of conception. In her mind's eye she went through the motions of the beginning of the girls' life. How they started as a single cell, which mysteriously split, most likely on day three, into two identical cells, continuing both to split and divide. They would have been two perfect seeds of life, moving towards their final nesting place, her womb. On day seven, their implantation would have been considered the first official day of pregnancy. A pleasing thought.

April got up to make herself a coffee. She waited for the splutter of the espresso machine, deep in thought. With the steaming cup in hand, she wandered over to the full-length windows that looked onto the garden. Two squirrels were chasing each other, followed closely by Alfie's gaze, their neighbour's ginger cat who was sitting on the tin roof of the shed.

She turned around to go back to her desk, saying to herself *what are you going to do in these seven days April? What will your offering be for Kenji's return?* The thought of Kenji gone, and of his return, re-activated her anger.

April took a moment to catch herself. *Instead of resentment*, she thought, *how about I do something with my anger. Write. A story a day. A story about a woman.* She felt a tingle. *A woman is a seed of life of sorts, a container for life force. She can be in touch with the potential and the death of existence. And she can grow humans.*

April pricked up her ears. *Seven women. Seven sisters of sort? I've always wanted a sister*, she thought with a little sadness. *I've always wanted to be in the middle of a huddle of women, their laughter and noise, an energy far reaching, holding hands in solidarity.*

Sometimes April imagined all her female patients holding hands. Sharing their stories. Stories April listened to in the cocooned tranquillity of her therapeutic space. A space curated for imagination, her safe space, her first child. A space where she was a mother to herself and to her patients' stories, that were asked to be held, remembered, made sense of, deconstructed and put back together again.

Most of her patients were women. Their stories often about how to survive in the web of relationships, yearning to thrive. Oftentimes caught in expectations in the eyes of others, that became their own. A woman's own mother never far away, often blamed, the relationship fraught with guilt and frustration, a sense of duty and solidarity too. Fathers, in comparison, got off lightly.

April's anger spiked again. She believed that relationships between women, good or bad, were overshadowed by male privilege. The rage of this morning, Kenji's absence, moved into sharp focus once more. It felt like a spinning wheel of fire. April lamented the fact that despite her best efforts, in part she had recreated a similar family set-up to that of her childhood.

Then as now, there was a busy man travelling around for

work, whilst the woman was tasked with holding together the family back home. Her father's need for professional status, had always taken precedence over the needs of the family, even if it meant that things were falling apart. Which they were. Her mother had spent most of the days' hours in her dark room, increasingly reaching for a drink to numb the unbearable. *At least Kenji's job is at the service of art*, April thought, *and for that, he is half-forgiven.*

In many ways Kenji was a very different man to her father. He was quiet and reflective and had always been supportive of her choices. He had grown up in Osaka, Japan to dedicated parents who were both artisans and teachers. Kenji moved to Europe and became a successful artist and later, when the twins were born, became an art curator. First attracted to Kenji's quietness, April later felt challenged by what she saw as a lack of expression.

In contrast, her father was loud and controlling. He had always demanded her mother's subservience, which he increasingly demanded of April, once her mother became ill. Whenever she was in his vicinity, as a child, and as an adult, April felt engulfed by a dark force she had to work hard at escaping. Considering herself a single child, April saw herself abandoned to living in the shadows of her brother's death. Memories of that time were a little hazy, but she knew for certain that it was an unhappy time.

There was a changing point however, that she remembers clearly. It was her 8th birthday. The day's strained celebration with her parents was brief, followed by her spending the rest of the day in her room. She was sitting on the deep window ledge watching the world go by, which is something she would do for hours. At some point, she thought she had fallen asleep and was dreaming as she saw a group of angel-like creatures hovering in the branches of the London Plane tree opposite. She remembers pinching her arm to ascertain if it was real or not. Then she saw their neighbour Bruno take his dalmatian dog Stardust for a walk and they waved at each other. When she returned her gaze to the tree, the angels were still there.

From that day, her perception was inhabited by creatures with ambiguous shapes. While she never saw the group of angels in the tree again, one such angel-like creature remained, accompanying her to different locations. The big slide in her local park, the supermarket round the corner, at the school gates, and at her friend Nancy's house. When it was hovering above their apartment block it was pulsating a soft pink.

April never told her mother about this but often thought that the apparition had come for both, as a protection and comfort for their broken hearts.

Her mother, having grown up in the shadows of the Catholic church, was staunchly anti-religious, and had no time for anything mystical. April often had an urge to pick her up and cradle her like a child, to soften her steely armour. Her mother had made two life changing trips out of Ireland, one to Liverpool for an abortion, and one to leave Ireland for good to move to New York where she lived with an aunt. It was there she met and married April's father. They later settled in London, where her father began his career as a plastic surgeon.

My mother, April thought, *has been scarred by life, but really scarred by the cruelty of 1950s Ireland that treated women harshly.* April's father was both emotionally and physically absent. *And unapologetically egotistical, which I cannot forgive him for*, April thought, *especially because society continues to forgive him every single day.*

April left home as quickly as she could. Since money had

never been an issue, she could study wherever she wanted. And although her father wanted her to study medicine, in the end he accepted her choice of studying fine art. *It was the art residency in Rome which broke me*, April thought, *and with that my love for the art world*. And at the same time, it was Rome and Kenji in it that replaced her brokenness with creativity as a philosophy of life, that both she and Kenji shared. April thought back to those summer evenings when she and Kenji sat on the city walls for hours talking, on top of one of the hills, with views like a film set, Rome beneath their feet.

April's attention swivelled back to the present. She looked at the sky, for a moment imagining it was a Roman instead of a London sky. Alfie the cat was still in their garden, stretching in a sunny spot amongst the buttercups. April did not want to think about Rome, nor how much in love they were back then, instead she wanted to focus on her new idea of writing stories.

There was a loud knock on the door. Their doorbell had broken a while ago, and Kenji, being good with his hands had crafted a decorative wooden door knocker. April was pleased the postman was using it as intended. The package contained a long-awaited vintage book on plant medicine of Ireland with a small section dedicated to the history of women healers and midwives of both births and deaths. April had been interested in ancient Irish healing traditions for a while intrigued by the fact that knowledge was passed down the female line at the service of the community. Scorned by the establishment, these women were later persecuted and often accused of witchcraft.

Of the little that her mother had shared about her Irish ancestry she did say that the family folklore mentioned healers in the distant past. Whether true or not April liked the idea, wondering whether her visions of the angels, was a gift from her Irish foremothers.

She had foreseen her twins before they were born, not as babies but as young girls, and that vision was true to reality once they came of that age. April had always felt that Aya and Sora were kindred spirits of her maternal lineage. Aya had a strong love of plants, from when she was little pointing them out, propelling April to learn about their medicinal qualities. Sora had an unbending sense for justice and equality, always thinking about alleviating other people's suffering, saying from a young age that she wanted to become what she called a 'helper'. Grounded and wise beyond their age, the health visitor who came to see them after their birth declared "they have been here before".

April leafed through the new book, looking for flowers that blossomed in the early Summer. She wanted to find a picture to inspire her creative process today. She found one that pleased her eye, yellow and shiny, called the Marsh Marigold, found in soggy ground, near stream margins and bogs. *This will do* April thought, applying clips to the side of the book so she could prop it up against the window.

Looking at the Marsh Marigold, her heart softened, and she thought *I am jealous of Kenji, and my jealousy is fuelled by my loneliness. His self-contained silence makes me feel abandoned. Kenji, born of makers and learners, is connected to the alchemy of change whereas I grapple with ghosts in empty landscapes.* April continued *I am also jealous because Kenji is a man, which comes with liberties and privileges not afforded to me as a woman. There is a silent violence against us women. And we always deal with the crisis.*

Like the twins' near-death experience when they were

three. Blue lighted to the hospital in the dark of the night they were burning up with a high fever. A terrifying 24 hour roller-coaster where Aya and Sora took turns at being very unwell. The doctors had feared the worst. When they suddenly got better, sitting up in their beds giggling, and eating mountains of food, they were unceremoniously discharged, none the wiser. In those couple of days of life and death April had existed in a parallel dimension. She remembers seeing everything in vivid colours; ink blacks, with edges of deep indigo, suffused by burnt orange of saffron in moments of hope.

She thought she was going to lose her mind. Especially since Kenji was away on business, his hurried return beset with cancellations and freak weather events. He only reached them when the crisis was over. *I don't think I've ever forgiven him for that,* April thought. That same month her mother died of a heart attack.

From the ordeal with the girls, she was left with a tremor inside that to this day had never really subsided. From her mother's death she was left with a profound relief followed by a calm like the sea after a storm.

April marvelled at tremor and calm, sitting side by side, demanding her attention.

From her brother's early death to the near death of her daughters, to the unexpected death of her mother, April could have done without it all. And yet, death had become a teacher. Death had left her with a vulnerability and at the same time with a power. Like how it felt being a mother.

The mother as a figure, as an experiencing being is central to it all April thought. *My mother's struggles to mother me and having to learn to mother myself has been formative. Being a mother and at the same time a daughter and a woman unfold between vulnerability and power.*

April thought about her ancestors. She had come across the idea of mitochondrial DNA imagining the qualities of vulnerability and power encoded in it. Mitochondrial DNA gets passed down from mother to child, changing little from one generation to the other, and can only be transmitted through the female line. Not fully understanding this April found it nonetheless intriguing, perhaps hopeful. She imagined a female ancestor passing her mitochondrial DNA of resilience and power down the line like a burning staff. Her ancestor in her imagination was a believer, a doer, a woman of the earth, who knew how to survive, but more so knew how to thrive.

Let her emerge from the ashes, April thought. *It is through her, the ancestral mother, that I may find my love for my mother. And her love for me. Ultimately, my love for myself. My strength, my body, my existence as the centre point.*

With that thought April jotted down some rules. Each story should have a thousand words she decided. And once the story was written she would draw and cut out a paper woman who would embody that story and the qualities therein.

The next day April felt buoyant. She felt the deep satisfaction that comes from creating. Today, she was going to see her supervisor, after which, she would start on the second story weaving the writing in between clients and the girls. As she cycled up the hill on her way to supervision, she peeled her eyes on the crest, anticipating the long tree lined descent. April loved the sensation of flying that came with speed. She took this route every two weeks, drinking from the uplift, no matter what the weather. There was something generous about the view at the top and the knowledge of the snaky river at the bottom, hiding behind buildings.

April on her bike, felt human, rather than gendered, where her strength and her sense of adventure amalgamated into something abiding.

The up-and-down-the-hill moment on her bike filled her with hope. Each time, a glimmer of it, rising in her heart, as she reached the top, in the split second of the transition from effort to effortlessness. Born that day, April wished to catch the rare sight once more, gliding by on the river Thames, having only seen it once.

April had been on the top floor of the library with a window seat, having been immersed in Paul Klee's Notebooks over several weeks, that had evoked an atmosphere of such beauty and completion, capable of answering all the questions she may have ever had about herself and the world.

Looking out that day she had caught a glimpse of a bellowing sail above and between the houses in the horizon. At first, she had disbelieved her eyes. A sight like a fairy-tale, a ship sailing the Thames that could not be fully seen but profoundly felt seemed improbable. The sighting made her so happy that it almost burnt her seams. And when the sail had disappeared behind the monolithic high-rise, she had lowered her gaze to Notebook I, where her eyes set on a line drawing of a fish.

In that moment, the sail joined up with the fish on the page in her mind's eye, the two images unifying into one, creating an anchor that settled inside of her with an as yet unknown meaning.

As April flew down the hill, there was no sail, unfortunately, but she had no time to mourn its absence. She stayed firmly in the middle of the street to avoid any impromptu car door opening. At the bottom she entered the fuming main road, meeting the dares of metropolitan traffic, weaving together the flow of careful movement and expansive contemplation.

Her thoughts turned to her supervisor, a beautiful soul she loved dearly, a sort of surrogate mother and fellow professional who did a great job at keeping April on an even keel. Whatever April was grappling with, professional or personal, Mabel was able to receive it, and April always stepped out of their encounters with more clarity. *She is old now*, April thought, and that thought unsettled her.

Then she thought, *what if I take a leap and close my practice? Become a writer instead*? Followed by another thought, *are Kenji and I made for one another*? She pushed that familiar one quickly aside.

As she approached the last major crossing, motor chaos and people morphed into rivers, intersecting and parting, tangling, and untangling as if dancing to a universal law. April felt a little wobbly and then she remembered a poem by Rainer Maria Rilke and she thought *beauty and terror, let everything happen to you.*

2

Rosa
Child

In the beginning there was light.
Rosa was told that she was born in a simple stone house high above the rocky outlines. Looking from below it looked like the house was touching the sky. It was the beginning of summer, and a sea of buttercups was carpeting the plateau in front of the house, nodding their heads in the gentle breeze. Rosa's mother told her that the stars and the moon were perfectly aligned the night before she was born. When she drew her first breath, light flooded the makeshift birthing room and she was caught by the confident hands of the local midwife, who took one cursory look at her and announced "she is fit and healthy. As strong as a goat".
Soon after, the midwife left to attend to another birth down the valley, a boy who unlike her was born barely alive. He died a few hours later. Her mother had always felt uneasy about this. The woman had been trying to conceive for a long time, and she remained childless thereafter.
Rosa's strength continued for much of her early childhood, reinforced no doubt by the presence of the mountains. She was inquisitive and lively. Like the sun that had greeted her

on her birthday, she had a luminosity that stood out.
Now in her late twenties Rosa only had a faint memory of the mountains.
What she was left with instead were echoes. The colour yellow prevailing, a shade that made her feel safe. Every year, with anticipation, she awaited the arrival of the shiny yellow petals of the buttercups, mingling with them with her bare feet. She'd often see a child's foot, from above, in her mind's eye, as if looking down on her own foot of her child self, broad and strong, resolutely placed on a rock, ready to climb. This image often went together with auditory echoes, a faint cheerful ringing of bells. Of the goats. Always goats. *They nimbly move about.*
A few years later they moved to the valley. Rosa remembers that things changed once they left, following her father's work as a geologist. Moving around the world felt unsettling. Rosa remembers becoming more reserved. Was it that her luminosity couldn't survive away from the mountains? Or was it how other people, her mother included, felt about her light? Once they had moved, to Rosa it seemed like there was no space for it. Adults seemed preoccupied and busy, always wanting something that Rosa did not fully comprehend. This felt dark to her. The more she grew the more she started to feel a discomfort around her light, and she eventually concluded that the light was not meant to be. Perhaps light was what children had and was something that adults left behind.
Adult life for Rosa was devoid of much joy and felt unsatisfactory in its greyness. Just as her luminosity came with discomfort as she grew older, the greyness now in turn made her feel uncomfortable too. It made her think of dangerous cliffs and rocks in the mountains, their sharp edges jutting out. Her thoughts kept attaching to a vague

story she remembered of a goat slipping off the cliff. In her head she could clearly hear the scraping noise of the hoof. She kept waiting for the thud of the goat's landing. What she heard instead was a long-drawn-out silence.

And this was precisely how Rosa increasingly felt, a silence that had no edges and no end. She decided to finally do something about it and go and see a therapist.

"Hello Rosa. Welcome. Have a seat. Take your time". Rosa nervously looked at the therapist allowing herself a moment to scrutinize her face. She had quite a few wrinkles, but her skin looked soft. Once she sat down, she registered the colour coral in the room. To the side of them both were big French windows looking out onto a wild garden. A welcome focal point for Rosa who felt awkward. *Where to begin*? she wondered. Now she was sitting here, this didn't seem like a good idea at all.

In the expectant silence, she could feel her chest tightening. Rosa saw mice running along the corridors of her ribs, all in one direction towards her heart. This made her smile, and she relaxed a little.

How should she begin? Rosa was familiar with her house of internal ghosts, and her dreams, soothingly accompanied by the presence of animals, big and small. This is how it's always been and was her best kept secret. Were she to let others in on this, there would be trouble, no doubt. Rosa shifted uneasily in the chair. Which was actually very comfortable. A big eared fortress of a throne that gave her shelter. She wriggled into it a bit more.

The therapist cleared her throat. Rosa stopped her wriggle. In a shot she saw bunnies scrambling over each other and quickly finding their burrow, the tail of the last one wriggling ferociously before it too disappeared.

"Rosa, why don't you tell me a bit about yourself?" Rosa

groaned inside. *A bit. About myself. Where to begin??* All she could see now were bolting horses galloping up the greenest of hills, and as they reached the top they came to a halt, their bodies quivering, nostrils flaring with the effort, looking out at the sea.

The image of the sea prompted her to start. "Well, I've been working on an oil rig for the last three years. The deep water scares me. I had to stop working there as I was very sad. Every day." Rosa felt that she was about to lose control over herself. The mice were now running away from her heart, all scrambling down her spine without arriving at her feet, which seemed essential. She felt suspended.

"Oil rig? That's an unusual work environment! Rough and burly." The therapist let out a clipped sound, almost like a laugh, which was like a thick rope slow motioning towards Rosa.

Rosa caught the rope. "Yes. It is. Very much. Burly. Like bears but without the softness." Rosa laughed freely now, which surprised her, and then laughed some more, which in turn made the therapist laugh.

Ah that feels better she thought. The mice have now all tumbled to the ground, as if someone had shaken them out of a bucket. They were now nestling around her feet. Rosa took a deep breath. "It was sad and scary. And now I feel lost. I feel like a fish out of water" she said quietly and shyly.

"The fish is scared of the water?" Rosa looked up and into the eyes of the therapist. Her eyes were calm, just like the sea the horses were looking at on the hill. "Hmm I see, yes, fish belong in the water but when the water is too deep you can't see them anymore. That's when it gets scary. And so, I am lost. But I've been feeling lost for a long time, perhaps even before the oil rig...."

The therapist did not look surprised. It was as if she knew

her story already. “Tell me more”. And so, Rosa began.
“I’m not sure this is right. But I keep thinking I need to be witness to her death. I keep seeing the goat dead at the bottom of the rocks. It’s not the fact she died. Although her death was sad, she was a happy goat, and she died doing what she did so happily, climbing and hopping on the rocks – frolicking on the plane with all the others. It’s that I didn’t hear the sound of her death. The lack of sound is suspended in my mind, and everything is jumbled up. I am confused.
“Start somewhere in your childhood. What can you tell me?” The therapist spoke kindly.
“I was always told that I was a happy and strong child. When I look back, I see everything in yellow happy hues. I touched the sky with my enthusiasm, like the house I was born in, seeing it as you come over the hill with its roof reaching into the blue sky. The happiness and enthusiasm have been lost on me for a long time. I feel shame for the happiness I once had, and I feel shame for having lost it.
Rosa continued “it is the long and numerous car journeys of my childhood that loom large in my memory. I hated the plasticky smell of the car mingled with the fumes of the motorway. It made me feel sick, small and insignificant. As we snaked through the car-clogged valley, I felt intimidated by the tallness of the mountains that I loved so much high up. There was something dark and immovable about them. They seemed to confirm existence as it is without me having a say in it”.
Rosa paused for a moment, checking the therapist was still listening. She was.
“In those early days, I felt more comfortable close to the ground, on my own terms, observing the minutiae of the ants’ journeys, looking at how the twigs and pebbles had landed by coincidence, forming landscapes I understood,

at a scale I could take in. At a scale where I was big, and they were small. It was the enduring presence of nature that helped me confront life as it was. Something about humans seemed unsatisfyingly unpredictable or predictable as it were. It made me feel empty and this spread like the morning fog in October, occasionally shift shaping into an opening. A hole through which the sun could reach, providing a little more focus for feelings like fear or sadness.

The fir trees across the road from our house where we eventually settled for a while, during the year a muted presence, called to me in the wintry months. Their branches drooped with the heavy weight of the snow, an unfair burden, it seemed to me. I went to brush the snow off the lower branches. They snapped back into a fluid, swaying movement, grateful so it seemed, releasing a spray of snow like a thousand particles. Glistening in the sun, it was showering down on me, my skin ready to receive. I felt a little glimmer of happiness, for the tree, for me.

I spent a lot of time on my own. I remember how I used to step from one flag stone to another all the way around our building block, stopping frequently to survey the landscape, to sniff the air and the musty smell of the undergrowth. Trekking over imaginary valleys and mountain ranges. It's the mountains that keep coming back to my mind. I am not sure anymore whether they are threatening or comforting. I know they were my friend when I was little. I was born nestled between them; the sharp edges lived side by side with the green of the grass. I was the mountains, and they were me.

"There is a contrast between the unfathomable depth of the sea and the concreteness of the mountains?" The therapist asked, she was still there, still calm. Rosa considered the question. "Yes. I get queasy thinking of the water, the

rolling waves...." Rosa brings her hands to her head, snakes slithering down her limbs, spinning fast.
"It makes your head spin." The therapist's voice brings the snakes to a standstill. Rosa thinks of the North Sea and the times when they visited her father's relatives. "It was freezing on that beach of my father's childhood. We spent hours on those vast beaches, with my cousins, emptied of the water for miles. We eased into the folds of sand and puddles, the wind rattling our bodies, our hair flying, swept clean. I found this hand sized smooth stone, purple, with a white streak across its body, shaped like a liver. This is mine I declared at the time, and I held onto the stone for many years. It's strange but that stone made me think of my mother, it felt like it was protecting me, spelling me into a good future" Rosa stops.
"A reminder of the rocks in the mountains?" The therapist asked and Rosa agreed by nodding and holding the therapist's gaze.
Rosa continued "The thing is, when you reach the top of the mountains above the tree line, something gives way to sky and space. You leave the tight feeling of the valley behind. There is choice and perspective. Different vistas are revealed, as you keep going up, and you do, even if you are tired, because you want to see more. As you emerge from the woods before the rocky bits, you get to be with the boulders, the moss draws you in and little streams emerge here and there. There is a purity up there. The colours bounce off each other, satiated green of the meadows against the yellow buttercups singing against the blue sky".
Rosa becomes quiet for a little while. When she begins to talk again her voice is more strained.
"There were moments I wanted to give myself over to the dark sea and be done with life. A week earlier, on the

mainland, I found a dead blue tit on the road. It made me incredibly sad. I picked it up, and seeing it nestled in my hand, dead, it seemed at the same times so alive in its vibrancy. I couldn't understand how this could be so. It was the harsh calling of the geese gathered every dawn on the rig, when my layers began to unravel. The hum of habitual unrest slowly giving way to a different sort of sensing. At the same time, I was getting angrier and angrier with the harsh sound of the geese, seeing myself bolting towards the horizon on the vast empty beach.

"Solid ground." The therapist says. Rosa looks at her. "Yes, solid ground". "Like your beginnings. They were solid?" The therapist asks. "Yes, they were". Rosa replies, and in her mind's eye she sees a slippery shiny baby. And then curled up, a warm downy ball like the blue tit, but alive, asleep in God's invisible hands. Smelling of apricots and chocolate. Rosa then says, "It seems like my body was embalmed with the beyond, born into the fitting environment of the mountains." Rosa pauses and holds her breath. Then she says, "I need to go back". Rosa looks at the therapist who looks back at her with an open face. "Finding your way back home. Inside and out. Something about solid ground, and the colour yellow. You the child, sturdy and strong". The therapist says slowly. Rosa smiles. She sees a goat kid leaping in the air, kicking all four legs, bleating. There is a faint ringing of the bells. Rosa says, "I feel like the me as a child has never really left me, but I feel that she can't be amidst the adults of this world". *And the animals*, she thinks silently, *don't share this yet with her*, a louder inner voice says.

"What were the adults in your life like?" The therapist settles into her chair as if preparing for the long haul. "My mother was kind but often sad, and my father was busy working as a geologist in far-away places. I guess it was he who eventually dictated the course of our lives. We followed him around the world. And those mountains became a distant memory. It seems like happiness never really returned after that. My mother wanted more children, but my father didn't seem that interested. Perhaps she had a few miscarriages, I don't really know". Rosa felt tired now. She looked out of the window. A fox lay curled up like a cat on a pile of leaves. *How can that be comfortable*, Rosa wonders. The fox made her think of the times spent in the haystacks, high up in the barn at her friend's farm. She remembers how the hay poked her bottom and legs, so uncomfortably, but the smell so intoxicatingly comforting. In that barn she could let her legs dangle, and her thoughts wander, to the mountain path behind the house, the sun as it came up behind the rocks, touching the tip of the trees further down. The loud chirping of the sparrows. She remembers the delight when mother cat finally had given birth to five kittens. How motherly she felt towards them, born that day in the hay.

She had a particular fond memory of the cherry harvest. The juicy black balls, growing in clusters, beaming, and greeting hands and mouths with delight. Filling countless baskets strapped to her growing body, a happiness inside her chest almost exploding, like the flock of birds shooting up into the sky when their feast was interrupted. The sun was moving in and out of the clouds, and the soft chattering of the others immersed in this simple activity of gathering, made her feel safe. Together and alone. Rosa loved being in the tree, playing queen surveying her land, her makeshift wand whooshing satisfyingly as she sliced it through the air. Yes, defying gravity, that's what she wanted to do as a girl, to fly and see the world from above. Rosa thinks *it's time to leave the hay and watch the milk come out of the*

udders. Time to feed the chickens. Time to go to sleep. And dream. Stars twinkling. Visions of ghosts, swirling around the room, waking my senses and lightening my sleep.
Rosa suddenly felt self-conscious as she realises that she had been miles away. She is back in the room with the therapist. She looks at the therapist whose presence is unchanged. Rosa notices once more the colour coral which she faintly registered when she entered the room. Now she sees it's the colour of the wall behind the therapist, repeated by the almost transparent curtains swaying softly.
In this moment, unspoken and unspeakable, Rosa is touched by something. And this something gives way to a space inside of her. *Perhaps things will be ok* she thinks.
"It's all in the stones" Rosa says out loud. "Stones tell the truth. That's why I've always loved pebbles as a child. Those little ones. You know, when you grab a fistful, and you drop them into a container with water, their greyness transforms into multiple colours that only the water can reveal. Suddenly it feels like they are coming alive, telling you stories. Suddenly things seem possible, expansive. As a child I thought that a small pebble grows into a big stone, like the one I found on the beach. Liver shaped, and smooth".
The therapist looks at Rosa. The light in the room has changed to a soft hue of pink. The fox Rosa saw in the garden sleeping on a pile of leaves has now woken up and takes a stretch. The therapist follows Rosa's gaze and says "Oh, that's our neighbourhood fox. He comes into the garden every afternoon. He has only three legs". They both look at the fox as he yawns. Indeed, he has only three legs and his tail is a sorry sight. It briefly looks in their direction, then runs off. So fast you wouldn't know that one leg was missing.

"Can I come back next week?" Rosa squints at the therapist.
"Yes, of course you can" the therapist says whilst rising from her chair. *Much wobblier than the fox, even though she has all her legs* Rosa thinks. For a moment it looks like the therapist is going to step towards Rosa. Instead, she steadies herself, smiles at her and says, "Let me lead the way".
When Rosa steps outside into the road a stunning strip of evening colour spreads across the darkening sky. *Shades of coral.*

3

Betty
Mother

Betty woke up startled.
For a moment she was not sure where she was. Then she remembered. It was Thursday and one week into her stay on this deserted island at the edges of the Atlantic Ocean. Which meant her time here was coming to an end. She needed to arrange for her return journey to the mainland today.
As usual, her thoughts started running riot in her head as soon as she woke. These days she rarely tried to get back to sleep, opting instead for getting up no matter what time. It was freezing cold, and she quickly slipped her layers on over her pyjamas, finishing with two pairs of woollen socks. In the main room she peered at the clock on the wall and could just about make out that it was 5am.
She moved towards the window, the darkness of the outside pushing in, a presence she quietly learned to appreciate in this place. Its inky blue quality felt calming. Gusts of wind were hitting against the stones of the croft, echoes reaching through the thick walls.

Betty fumbled through the dark to the little entrance hall where she reached for her coat, hat, and gloves. It took a good while to put them on in the right way, but she slipped effortlessly into her wellies. As she opened the door, she was hit by the cold wind. She took a sharp breath, and stepped out, grateful for the thick gorse that sheltered her for a few steps before reaching the vast expanse of the beach.

As soon as she was out in the open, its exposure, each time, a little frightening, the full force of the wind unsteadied her body. She had to find her balance, before leaning into it with a resolute march. The horizon was almost indistinguishable from the rest of the landscapes, with the tiniest sliver of a lighter shade far away. The sea was roaring. Betty felt the same roar inside as she was battling the elements, quickening her step as best as she could, rushing towards the water with all her might.

Once she was close to the sea, she veered sharply left towards the rocks, which stood facing inland in a semi-circular enclosure, a perfect rudimentary shelter. She knew exactly where she needed to sit to find the indentation her body had made on the previous days. With a thud she lowered herself and sighed with relief, the journey from the croft to here seemed to have taken a lifetime. She wriggled into her coat, folding deep into her body.

Her gaze settled east, *in attendance of the sunrise,* nature's daily morning prayer. She had discovered that this daily ritual of braving the elements and waiting for the new day quietly with no expectation brought a stilling to what seemed a lifetime of riotous thoughts. The elements were mirroring her internal voices, of which there were many, but the turning of the wheel from dawn to dusk with its consistent phases was settling her in its predictability.

As the horizon burst into a dramatic burnt orange, Betty began to think about her impending departure. She didn't want to go. She was surprised how comfortably she had settled into this solitude, something she had not been sure of when she had first come here. What she had discovered was a quiet internal feeling, that was still stretching. An unfamiliar sensation that felt important. She didn't want to lose it, this brave new counterpart to her usual rioters in her head.

The sunrise orange slowly gave way to a grey strip suffused with light blues. Betty got up to walk along the shoreline. She wanted to saviour the beach with every cell of her body. All week long she had been almost alone apart from a dog walker or two. The relief she felt from the absence of social chit chat was profound.

Lost in her thoughts Betty suddenly heard an unfamiliar sound behind her, a sort of arhythmical thumping she could not place. Her heart jumped and as she swivelled around, she saw a small herd of white horses galloping towards her. They were slowing down, then came to a standstill, the first of the group barely five feet away from her, with flaring nostrils, looking her straight in the eye.

Betty felt panic rising. She broke into a cold sweat, feeling the urge to rip her coat open to give space for breath, but she was too scared to move. She had always been terrified of horses. For a moment Betty felt like she was being swept away from underneath the ground, like a wave pulling her out at sea. She wanted to scream but her voice was cut off.

Next thing she knew, a person appeared nearby. It was a rugged old man with a bright red cap. He was stretching one arm towards her saying 'it's ok' and at the same time with his other arm he was waving the horses off, making clicking sounds with his throat. The horses shook their heads, manes flying, and trotted away towards the water.

Betty started to shake and at the same time she registered the scene in front of her, breathtakingly beautiful. The sun had just broken through a thick sheet of cloud, transforming the grey water into a peacock of aliveness, deep indigo, with turquoise layers. The white sand and the white horses next to the sea looked majestic and pristine. Then the sun disappeared. Aware of the man still standing next to her, Betty suddenly felt exposed and engulfed in shame.

Betty looked at him and mumbled "I am sorry. I feel silly. I am very afraid of horses. I did not expect them here". "No problem" the man said. He looked at her with just a little hint of curiosity. "Lovely day" he said. Betty nodded. It was his curious gaze that tipped Betty over. It felt intrusive, and although Betty felt grateful for his help, at the same time, she started to feel angry. This magical arch of solitude, of just her and her thoughts, now shot to pieces by this.

Betty felt hot rage rising, taking hold of her tummy, and moving up her body fast. Any second it was going to spill out, which Betty desperately wanted to avoid. She forcefully bit her lower lip, tasting blood in her mouth. She swilled around, walking quickly away from the man. She felt nauseous and all she could think of was to get back to the safety of the croft. As she arrived, she crashed into the house, kicked off her wellies, ripping her coat, hat, and gloves from her body impatiently. An animal-like sound came from her throat and tore through the silence. Betty brought one hand up to her heart as heaves of sobs rolled over her body. She slid to the floor with a heavy thump as her limbs gave away.

Betty was lying on the ground for a long time. She watched a fat spider crawl lazily across the floor, disappearing through the cracks about halfway across the room. Apart from the ticking of the clock and the faint sound of the wind and waves, all was quiet. Beams of light flooded the room on and off as the sun moved westward, in and out of the clouds. Betty could hear the cry of a buzzard, urgent and purposeful, her own breathing shallow and faint.

Soaring high, the buzzard circled above the house a few times, then flew towards the sea, cruising across the beach until it settled on a lone tree where the island was jutting out.

Betty missed the slot for booking her return ferry. Not that she was thinking about that. At some point she found herself on the sofa, even though she had no recollection of when she got up from the floor. There she wrapped herself into the woollen blankets, watching the changing sky, until dusk set in.

Eventually, she decided to get up. She warmed up some soup but found that after one spoon she didn't want it anymore. She lit the fire and went back to the sofa. *How did I get here?*

Betty felt confused, and yet she also had a sense that she had come full circle. From the darkness of the morning to the darkness of the night, the passage of time had delivered her into a different dimension. What had happened on the beach earlier seemed from the distant past. It was as if there had been a before and after, the before looking terribly chaotic and restless. Betty sat up with her arms wrapped around her legs. The wind was howling, but inside the croft she felt safe and protected.

She started to think about her mother and how much her mother had struggled as a single mum. The thought of her mother never came without thinking of Betty's siblings. How her mother needed Betty to mother the younger ones, a need so strong it gave Betty no choice. Unlike the other children, Betty was spared the cold indifference her mother increasingly felt towards the children as they fell on hard times. There were too many mouths to feed. All Betty seemed to do was work hard, whilst watching her mother disappear.

She thought back to her mother's funeral many years ago when her own children were still little. In her retirement years her mother had returned to the seaside town of Portrush in Northern Ireland, which was not far from her mother's sister and where they had grown up. Her mother got ill soon after and died within the year. Betty had travelled from England to the funeral, booking a modest hotel that wasn't too far from the beach, remembering how worried she was about how much it would cost.

She remembers how ravenous the children had been the day after traveling, wolfing down the starchy breakfast, a rare treat, served up by a tired dinner lady who matched the lacklustre dining hall. There were two wooden eagles on plinths flanking the French windows, which her youngest eyed suspiciously. In contrast to the children's excitement about the novelty of it all, Betty had felt suffocated by the stuffiness of the hotel made worse by her thoughts of the impending funeral. She imagined throwing the windows wide open, the two magnificent birds coming alive, and carrying her into the sky.

Of the funeral itself she could remember little, just that there was a gaping absence of feelings. She remembers the ramshackle rowing club where the wake was held, and her

frequent trips to the beach with the kids, when the stench of beer and smoke was getting too much.
Etched in her memory was a moment of the children playing happily by the water, giving Betty a welcome break to catch her breath. Surveying the scene in front of her she had noticed an old fishing boat to her left. It had occupied a quiet space. The twilight, with its purple-orange light courting the mottled grey descending on the scene, had an alluring dream-like quality. The crashing sound of the incoming waves had been deafening, interspersed with the delightful squeals of the children who had been trying to avoid getting wet. Several black plastic bags stuck to the mast of the fishing boat, had been fluttering noisily in the wind. She remembers thinking that from afar they looked like ravens, engaged in a ritualistic dance for the dead.
With her awareness back on the sofa in the croft, Betty re-arranged the blankets. Thinking of her mother, brought longing. A yearning for the love of a mother, a clean sort of love that didn't need to be earned, that didn't come with hard work. She can't remember her mother ever saying I love you, or holding her, or touching her with tenderness. Touch was always a transaction; it was about what Betty could do for her.
Betty shifted uneasily on the sofa, bringing both her hands up to her chest remembering the pain she felt this morning when she crashed to the floor. A throbbing pain with intermittent pierces, like arrows, was now returning. There had been little joy growing up in their household. Betty started to cry. It felt as though the yearning Betty had for her mother could never be stilled. It seemed like the same sort of yearning she had for the sea, the shells, pebbles, crab carcasses, and the driftwood, washed clean

and smooth, the disappearance of which at high tide could never be stopped. And yet, in this place, Betty had felt some form of safety all week, held by the beauty of the beach and the sea, she had started to appreciate the water like a surrogate mother, transmitting trust that the coming and goings of the tides was how things were meant to be.

The disturbance this morning was like a cut that threw her back into the chaos of her thoughts and painful feelings. Thinking of it now, Betty could see fear and pain like a disembodied entity, hovering in its darkness. It felt a bit like when she saw her mother dead on the bed the day before the funeral. It was revelatory. It was clear that with the absence of spirit, all that was left was a cold, hard shell, which is how her mother appeared to Betty when she was alive. The warmth of her body piercing Betty with its unattainability.

Betty's mothering was different. With a safe distance away from mothering her siblings, which had never felt right, she marvelled at her own children's existence, and she was relieved to find that it was easy to love them. Betty remembers their tiny feet and hands, their rosy cheeks, and their happy voices. The noise they made, tumbling over each other like puppies. Betty loved them generously and held them firmly. And yet, perhaps over time, Betty wonders, was she holding on to them too hard?

She wiped her tears away, pulling the blankets tighter around her body. *This was a long time ago now. That sort of mothering a distant memory. That sort of mothering that softens the heart most easily.* Now that her children have grown and gone their own way, she is fighting off a cold feeling in her heart, their departure reminding her of her mother's distance. Betty did not want to allow that cold feeling because she knew how wrong that feeling feels.

Then there is the small matter of being a girl Betty thought. Despite enjoying dolls and their domestic world, despite wanting to mother and tend with care her own children, she remembers not wanting to be a female. She always thought that there was no advantage to be had from being a girl. The memory of her brothers' confidence vivid, their laughter and snigger, their doing as they pleased. Which she as a girl could not. They had always had the power to set the tone.

This was a far cry from the shame and embarrassment she experienced from being a girl, the world of bodily changes and emotional roller coasters. Somehow, it had always been made clear to her, it was her job to contain the messy stuff. Besides, it had always been obvious that her mother preferred the boys.

With that last thought Betty swiftly got up from the sofa. Her eyes set on the bucket next to the fireplace. She grabbed it roughly and hurled it across the room with a deep throated bawl. Betty was trembling from the surge of rage and its discharge, and for a moment crouched down onto the floor to steady herself. She then walked back to the wood burner and put some more logs onto the dying fire, the growing light and warmth settling.

Betty's thoughts circled back to the day of the funeral. That morning, after breakfast, together with one of her sisters, they had gone down to the beach to give the kids some play time before getting them to sit through the rituals of church and burial. She later managed to escape for a quiet walk along the promenade, remembering the deserted arcade, where a piece of wrapping paper was swept along by a gust of wind. Betty came across an empty art gallery and remembers how indulgent it had felt to go inside. She walked through the gallery with a purposeful gait, scanning the works as she went, as if looking for something specific. And there it was, a pencil drawing of a landscape entitled *The Rapeseed Harvest.*

Betty had paused to let the drawing impress itself on her, as she travelled in her imagination to the harvested field, standing in the middle of it. It was barren, yet attractive. The just-harvested, bright-yellow rapeseed flowers seemed still visible, shimmering like phantoms above the shorn off stems. The stalks that were left behind, bereft of their golden glow, stood proud and upright. Something about this drawing spoke to Betty, perhaps about what was to come, and she remembers leaving the gallery strengthened.

When she returned to the beach her youngest was waiting for her. Nestling into her lap as she sat down, she framed her face with her soft hands and said "I love you mummy" while letting out a deep sigh. Betty whispered in response, and she repeated it now on the sofa in the croft *all shall be well, and all shall be well, and all manner of thing shall be well,* a famous quote by the female visionary Julian of Norwich, which Betty had adopted as her own mantra ever since she had come across it.

Betty smiled, thinking back to that moment of ease on the beach. The love expressed by children is pure, full, and expansive. *It mends broken hearts*. When they grew older, the girls expressed their love more subtly. Betty felt she had to be attentive to catch it. She might get a glimpse of a softening as it moved across their faces, across their eyes, evidence of a still kind of love that could not break. It occurred to Betty, that she had to come here to this deserted island, to be confronted with the fact of love, the loss of love, and the lack of love that tied her to the people in her life, past and present, no matter what. To Betty it seemed that there was no choice in matters of love.

Betty reflected that the man with the horses this morning had expressed an instinct so natural of protection and love, it had broken her heart open. It had brought her up close to her mother, the daughter in her and in turn the mother to her own self and children, and how this complicated tangle of daughter, mother, daughter had precipitated her towards this breakdown. She still did not want to go back home. Yet she had to. Even though her adult children did not need her anymore she still needed to fulfil her role of being the mother, just in case and, nonetheless.

Betty was just about to get up from the sofa to make some tea when she heard a faint knock coming from the door. At first Betty thought it was the wind, but then a louder knock followed. She felt a little scared, pricked her ears, and then slowly moved towards the entrance hall. Hesitantly she opened the door. She just about recognized the man from the ferry port who was wrapped up warm with the wind tearing at this coat, his friendly face peeking out from his hood. She beckoned him in and quickly closed the door behind them. The silence that followed was awkward.

As he lowered his hood he peered into her face cautiously, clearing his throat, he said "Sorry to bother you Madam. Clyde with the horses told me you were up here, and he asked me to check on you to make sure the horses haven't frightened the wits out of you. He says he hopes you are ok. Also, weren't you meant to catch the Saturday ferry back? I can make sure there is a ticket for you ready." Betty couldn't speak at first. She felt quite overwhelmed.

She thanked the man for his thoughtfulness and was touched by the open-hearted kindness of Clyde who held no grudge about her running off without a word, sending this man instead to check on her.
Betty stumbled over her words as she tried to say some of this but then settled on saying "Would you like a warm drink? Or a whisky perhaps?"

*

Thanks to that late night visit Betty got her seat on the ferry back to the mainland on that Saturday morning. Her resistance about going back had lessened. The sun was out, and the sea was calm. The ferry was full and there was a jovial atmosphere. Somehow time stretched in a good way, allowing Betty enough space to sort through things in her mind.
She replayed the scene with the horses and Clyde many times. Sometimes it was his funny hat she saw. Sometimes the flared nostrils of the horse in front of her. Then the image of the smooth whiteness of the horses' fur, the way they stood as a group perfectly aligned with the white sand, found a place in her. When she shut her eyes, she saw the blue and turquoise of the sea, swooshing gently inside.
The transfer from the ferry to the train was smooth, as were the several short trips after. Once Betty settled into the longer journey south, she was delighted to realise that their train line crossed the river Clyde several times, passing a town called the Motherwell, which she had not noticed on her way up. A sense was settling inside, that all had its place, brought on by meeting the rivers' namesake Clyde that had opened her well of mother grief.

As the train approached her hometown, Betty had a moment of renewed agitation. Questions started bundling in, making her jittery like the deafening roar of the wind and the crashing of the waves. But then she steadied herself. Calm waters. Clyde. With a mothering sense of coming closer to home, she could see things more clearly. Looking back at her. Clyde's outstretched arm. The waving hand towards the horses. The look of care on his face.
As Betty stepped off the train a flock of pigeons shot up into the sky, and as she followed their flight, she caught a glimpse of a blinking advert that said *You have arrived, welcome home.*

4

Brigid

Ancestor

Brigid ran nimbly up the hill.
She was excited about reaching the top, anticipating the cusp, the fall into the view of the Atlantic Ocean, like an embrace, taking a seat at her place of divination, the rock next to the rowan tree. As she arrived, she came to a standstill, opening her senses wide. Her breathing, laboured from the rush, now began to calm down. Her body, hot from the walk, was welcoming the breeze that was brushing gently against her clothes and hair. The sea was reaching towards her with a sparkle. She heard the loud krak krak of the male corn crake, listening beyond to the busy hum of the bees.
Brigid exhaled. Walking over to the rock and tree she said *good morning rock,* touching the flat part closest to her, *and hello Rowan, my seer,* touching lightly its smooth bark. Brigid hopped onto the rock, lowering herself, belly down, facing the ocean, shuffling and settling until her body yielded into the indentation of the stone.
It was early summer, her favourite time. The air was full, the abundance of nature filling every gap in the atmosphere

with a density that was almost intoxicating. With her legs spread wide behind her, Brigid lay still, like an insect bathing in the sun. She scanned the landscape in front of her, catching glimpses of the sea between the undulating long grasses dotted with poppies and wild carrots, their snowy white heads swaying and dancing.

She began to meticulously survey the meadow, looking for the Mugwort patch, good for pain relief, cramp relief, and aiding digestion, the Sorrell, good for fevers, aiding digestion, an anti-inflammatory, and the Woundwort, antispasmodic and sedative, which was further down to her left. She was going to pick some of the best later. This patch of medicinal plants had been looked after by her foremothers and herself, harvesting only what they needed to bring relief to their families and communities.

Brigid was born with an innate gift for healing. Her mother and grandmother said that seven miracles preceded her birth and that the venerated goddess Brigid had appeared to them shortly after she was born, prophesizing her future as a healer. Initiated into the fold of the wise women healers in their community, young Brigid stood out with her special aptitude for tuning into nature and receiving answers. She learned by osmosis spending most of her time amongst the plants and trees. In a way, Brigid was brought up by mother nature with Saint Brigid watching over her.

Brigid was aware of the seriousness of ill-health and hunger that had been besetting their community for far too long now, unsure what the future was holding. She had come here today to find answers, to gather medicine, even though plants can't fill empty bellies. Brigid sat up on the rock and whispered *dear dandelion, cleanse their blood and tonify their body and mind, help the toxins exit their bodies. Oh, my dear comfrey, take their pain away. My cherished hawthorn, help them bear the pain in their hearts for we have lost so many.* Brigid took a deep breath while visualizing the elder tree near their house whispering with fervour *my sacred elder, my great mother, rid them of the heat in their bodies, please save them one by one.* She felt the weight of her prayer, the urgency of her call. Only one brother and one sister were left in her family; five of her siblings and most of the elders had perished. Many had moved to other places to better their chances, including her parents who had moved down south. Migration had become common, changing the landscape of her childhood beyond recognition.

Brigid felt chilly, as sorrow was reaching her heart. Dark clouds started to gather, and gusts of wind started to tug at the grasses and flowers, pushing them this and that way. A flock of crows took off, calling to her, ominously. Then the sun broke through the clouds once more, meeting the ocean with a defiant arm outstretched. The waves lit up, glittery ripples moving westward. Brigid's chilly body warmed up quickly and she began to feel lighter. While she focused on the crimson of the poppies, she started to feel sleepy. She lay down and invoked a dream that began by the river.

She stands in a clearing of a pine tree wood, spinning in circles, receiving a current of earth energy that moves up her spine, up the trunks of the pines, shooting up into the sky and beyond. She comes to a standstill in the shade of the trees, with a dancing pattern of light on the ground. There is stillness and commotion. Brigid hears the leaves rustle. The voice of the river is steady, washing over the rocks, lapping near the edges. Brigid feels happy. A softly pulsating yellow globe is radiating inside of her, an energy mirrored in the face of her mother and grandmother who stand nearby. A girl with thick black hair moves close to her, looking at Brigid intently with luminous blue eyes. Brigid watches her as she walks among a community of houses scattered across green hills. Small patches of cultivated land, interspersed by wild meadows teeming with flowers and wildlife, sprawl across the landscape. Suddenly, a storm rips planks of wood from houses, sending them flying together with the girl with the blue eyes. In quick successions Brigid sees happy communal moments to scenes of hardship. A snowstorm sweeps along the ridge of the mountain. Treetops appear faintly above bulging snow clouds. Brigid watches as women healers fight the storm, their clothes torn, fragments dissolving. Flashes of arctic-alpine plants appear and disappear. There is a sudden drop in temperature. Back by the river there is a deceptive sense of peace. The yellow globe hovers above Brigid and starts to spin, first counterclockwise then clockwise, a spinning wheel of fire, whipping up the waters on the bank. Brigid gets seized by a wave that pulls her into the river. Just in time she manages to get hold of the spinning yellow globe, drawing it swiftly into her body. The river is strong and pulls her under. She sinks, the spinning globe slowing down to a quiet pulse. Brigid, hovers inches above the river's bed where all is dark and quiet. She looks up from what now appears to be the bottom of the sea. She hears the frightful shouting of warring men on a ship. People are being killed and thrown into the sea, crimson clouds of blood spreading. A woman screams.

Brigid brought herself back to the present moment. She sat up and gazed out at sea. The invocation confirmed what she had sensed. Change was about to come. Soon the power of plant medicine would be usurped by the foolishness of warring men. Brigid sensed that if she wanted to survive, she may well have to leave soon. Even though leaving her homeland would break her heart, would uproot her power. For a moment Brigid contemplated a possible departure, seeing herself amongst a crowd of people on a ship, sailing towards an unknown future. *Just in case*, Brigid thought, *I'll gather eight yarrow leaves, to give me courage and protection, to ward off evil on my journey henceforth, whatever it may be.*

Brigid knelt on the ground, brushing gently over a few yarrows in front of her, plucking one that felt right. She looked at the flower and gave thanks. Then she picked the feathery leaves and wrapped them carefully in her handkerchief, tying it around her neck. Watching herself do this, seemed to confirm that her departure was close. She crumbled the flower head in her hand, inhaling the earthy smell, and slid the handful into the pocket of her skirt. She then snapped the stalk into little pieces and put them in her other pocket. Brigid got up, took a last look at her surroundings and ran down the hill, murmuring *yarrow, yarrow, lead the way.*

5

Stella
Fragments

It is Monday morning, and the doctors are doing the first ward round of the week. Stella stares into the eyes of a young male doctor "What did you say?" she asked. The doctor replied hurriedly "You were a beat away from dying. A couple of hours more and you would have died of blood poisoning". The doctor looks at her with impatience and a hint of accusation. She was unsure what to ask next, even though she had a million questions. The doctor appeared tired and seemed keen to move on. It had been a busy night at the Charité Hospital in Berlin. "A delay in the hospital handover today" the nurse informed her in a clipped voice when Stella insisted on some news earlier in the morning. All she knew was that she had been brought in by ambulance. She was found collapsed outside a bar in Prenzlauer Berg. The doctor was now giving instructions to a junior next to him. He turned back to Stella who was tracing vacantly the faint pattern of the hospital sheet "I can discharge you today as you responded well to the antibiotics. Make sure you finish the course and take it easy for next few days. You should be back to normal in about a week's time".

Back to normal in about a week's time. A beat away from death. Stella was bewildered. She had very little recollection of the past 24 hours. She tried to piece it together as she was waiting for the doctor earlier. She knew that she had been with Ryan, who had left the bar with another man. She had felt slightly put out by that. However, she was not sure whether they were at the bar yesterday or the day before. What she did know was that the past two weeks had not been good. She had been drinking more than usual, as well as taking some drugs.

A few hours later Stella stepped out of the hospital. Hit by the intensity of the city all she could think of was the comfort of her bed and the sparsity of her flat. Once back, Stella stripped naked, desperate to wash off the murky uncertainty of the past few days. She stood with relief under the hot shower until the bathroom was thick with steam, unfurling her tightness, sobs rippling through her body, like waves crashing. Once she felt emptied out, she began to inspect her body, looking for evidence of infection amidst a sense of groundlessness. Her index finger looked and felt strange. The tip was bright red with some white blotches. It looked swollen and it looked like there was a receding redness and some more blotchy skin radiating into her hand.

Stella stared at her hand. She had a strange sensation of looking at something that was detached from her, belonging to someone else. Fragments of body parts and disjointed memories. Then she remembered *I cut myself when I was trying to cook!* Slowly, the past events returned to her. She wrapped a towel around herself and gingerly walked to the kitchen. It was like an incriminating scene; cuttings of vegetables, the pungent smell of onions still in the air, dirty pans and plates, the stove stained, and plaster wrappers with splatters of dried-up blood all over the counter. *Ryan.*

I need to speak to Ryan. Stella felt panicky. She wanted to get her phone from her bag she had dropped at the entrance. Rummaging through its bottomless chaos, made her immediately tired. She stopped herself. *Perhaps not.* Instead, she went to bed.

Stella slept deeply and had two dreams. In the first she was floating down a river on a barge accompanied by six women, all dressed in white robes. Their presence was calm. She had a sense that they were going to show her something important. In the next dream she was giving birth to a baby who bit into her finger as soon as it was born. Her mother was there looking at her with piercing eyes.

Stella woke up in the late afternoon. *Shit, the antibiotics!* She stumbled into the kitchen and filled a pint glass with water, downing it in one go together with the tablet. She looked around and groaned. She couldn't bear the sight of the mess in the kitchen. She went to the living room. Then walked back to her bag to get her phone. Five missed calls from Ryan. One from her mother. Two messages from Petra. All worried about her.

She winced. *This is too much! I don't want to speak to anyone.* Anxiety gripped her, and she started to feel faint. She lowered herself on the floor and lay on her back, trying to breathe deeply. *How can I talk to anyone when I don't even know what happened. This is crap.......... Shit, shit, shit!* She rolled to her side, into a foetal position. This made her feel worse. She sat up sharply, hands flat on the floor. Then she remembered her dreams. She immediately thought of her mother, who would not be impressed with her. *That's what that stern look meant in the dream! This time I would deserve her scorn; I fucked up big time!* Stella started to feel sick again.

Leaning onto the sofa she grabbed her phone, staring at it

for a long time. She was angry with Ryan now. *Why the fuck did he leave me? Weren't we meant to stick together? This is typical of Ryan. He is such a selfish prick!* Stella swore some more, thinking of her mother again, who disapproved of her lifestyle and her fondness for swearing, which Stella loved doing with a passion. Swearing wasn't just a rebellion, it was a mode of expression that kept her firmly in the now, she who could disappear so easily. Stella remembered her mother only swearing once when she had misplaced her car keys in the fridge. The swear word came out of her mother's mouth, limp and clipped, and Stella remembers feeling fascinated with this rare expression of frustration. She had scrutinized her mother's face closely, wanting desperately to know more about the feelings behind her mother's cautious utterance.

The phone rang, which startled her, which made her drop the phone on her foot. *Fucking shit!!* It was Ryan. Their conversation was brief. Ryan asked why she hadn't responded to him since that night. She told him that she had come down with a cold and had been resting, which he believed. Ryan started to tell her about the guy he had left with. She asked tentatively "was I ok that night when you left?" He replied with surprise "Yes babe you were on fire, dancing away. Why?" She didn't respond other than saying it was nothing and that she was tired and needed to go.

Stella threw her phone onto the sofa and stared into space. She shook her head. *Is that it? If I don't say anything, he will not ask. And since I won't say, that's that!* She had never liked confrontation, which left her frustrated. She grew up learning not to say what she wanted or needed. Going along with the general mood was better, not being heard or seen felt like a small price to pay for the absence of conflict. *But this is the shit price that I pay for this shit-*

face coward that I am! Stella hit the sofa with her injured hand. She winced with pain. Not enough pain. She had an image of herself running against a wall smashing her head, repeatedly.
She thought about her dream again. The part with the baby was strange, an ugly little thing. Yet the baby biting into her finger seemed to talk about the finger that almost cost her life. Maybe it was a warning. *I'm such a baby that's what it means! I have to grow up! Seriously, dying at the age of 22 would suck!* And what about the six women on the barge? They seemed to be humming with an assured sense of power. This eluded Stella. No woman in her life was like that. To be perfectly honest, Stella was wary of women. In her opinion they lacked sincerity. And courage. And that included herself. *Maybe this is a wake-up call? A turning point. A sort of psychic death rather than an actual death.* Stella felt quite proud of this thought. It felt uncharacteristically mature and reflective. Not exactly qualities she was known for. Her friends got easily fed up with her for her multiple dramas, which usually involved her losing something or missing an important deadline or appointment. *Thinking about it, Petra is probably the only one who truly cares about me.* She was kind and saw the good in people. Stella made a mental note to ring her later. *Right*! She got up, defiantly. She marched into the kitchen, got a bin-liner "I'll deal with you later" she said out loud, pointing at the kitchen on her way out. Swiftly she walked into her bedroom, sweeping through the space with focus: into the bin went one opened and three un-opened packets of cigarettes, along with a stash of weed in the wooden bowl on her bedside table. Then she went back into the kitchen and grabbed the multiple packets of pain killers and anti-acid tablets. In they went. Reaching for her hoard of sour

sweets, she inspected them briefly then thought, *maybe actually, I'll keep* these, *despite mum, and they literally help me survive. "From* solids to liquids!" She yelled, opening the fridge and reaching for the cans of coke. She opened one after another, pouring the contents down the drain. An almost-full vodka bottle followed, as well as the half-empty gin bottle and some old amaretto that *no one ever wants to drink anyway!* Down the drain the sticky stuff went. She duty-fully put the cans and the bottles into the recycling bin and then started to tidy and clean the kitchen. She put the radio on and whistled along to the current tunes, feeling strangely cheerful. "This feels cleansing!" she shouted out loud, throwing her fists in the air and doing a little twirl. She almost fell over and had to steady herself. There was the nausea again.

By the time she was finished, the flat was gifted with a golden evening light. She walked through her space with satisfaction. Specks of dust danced in the air as the last bit of sun poured in, throwing jungle shadows on the wall, a replica of the only plant she kept alive, her Swiss cheese plant. Stella felt warm inside. She also felt weepy. Then she phoned Petra. It was an easy chat, but she didn't tell her about the hospital and about her brush with death. They came from similar backgrounds, which bound them together, but unlike Stella, Petra had always been quite proper, doing things the right way. Stella was worried that Petra might judge her for getting into this mess. Besides, she had a strong feeling that this was a secret to keep for a while. *Until I figure out what next.* There was something appealing about this unknowing transitional space. A gift in disguise *like when your computer crashes and you lose all your files. You think your life is over until you realise that they have been shit files in the first place.* Stella felt her anger rise again. *Fuck shit of a life! Fuck you, Ryan. Fuck you Berlin, I hate you! And fuck you and your women Dad! You made life a fucking misery!* Stella went into the bathroom and looked into the mirror. Her long hair was falling in scraggly tails over her shoulders, tired from going through many colourful transformations. Her thoughts turned to her recurrent fantasy of shaving her head. Would she dare this act of rebellion? Stick her finger up to the hyper feminine women of her childhood? Her mum with her carefully applied make-up and sensible kitten heels. Stella shuddered.

She started to search the bathroom cupboards for the trimmer her flatmate had left behind. "There it is!" she shouted triumphantly. She hit the on button and the whirring sound made her feel tickly all over. Excited and scared, she looked from the trimmer to her reflection, back and forth. After one last look at her worn-out hair, she caught a flicker in her eyes. She grabbed a fistful and made the first inroad close to the skull. Like feathers, her hair floated to the ground. When she was done Pixy like features looked back at her, which she liked. She took a deep breath and felt energized. She quickly got dressed and pulled her leather jacket from the cupboard. The one she had bought in the vintage market a few weeks ago but had been unsure about. "There, that's what this jacket was waiting for!" She grabbed her keys, looked at her phone and decided to leave it behind, and went downstairs to unlock her bike in the courtyard.

For all the loathing she felt towards Berlin right now she loved the fact that she could cycle everywhere. She did the short ride to Tempelhofer Feld, the disused airport with its vast fields and airstrips, her favourite thinking place, at high speed. She was an assured rider. Speed made her feel free, and she shot into the fields as if a plane herself, ready to take off. The atmosphere was peaceful, with a small crowd of evening lovers, enjoying the balmy air and the light breeze. The sun was preparing to treat everybody to a stunning set, lighting up the airstrip, golden pinked streaked arms receding into the horizon. Stella cycled into the fire with a beating heart. The wind on her shaven head and face. A yellow ball of happiness exploded in her chest. *I am free!* At the end of the airstrip, she turned around, cycling back the other way, towards the emerging darkness. Tears started to stream down her cheeks, as she leaned into the pedals hard. *I can be happy!* she said vehemently in her head. Pedalling harder. *And if I cycle fast enough to the end and turn around, I get to have another go at cycling into the light.* From East to West and back. Just as the sun was setting, she slowed down to a cruising speed. She started to think. *I need to be honest. I've been lying to myself, and I've been on the run.*

Living in Berlin had not felt like the right decision the moment she arrived, almost two years ago. But she couldn't go back on her decision. It would have felt and would have been seen as a failure. A rash decision so typical of hers. Thinking about the dream again she now saw that the six women were in direct opposition to the most significant six women in her life. Her mother, her nan, her two sisters, and her auntie with her daughter. Growing up she felt uncomfortable with how these women had set the tone. How they defined themselves through their preoccupation with men had always felt alien to Stella, who had always stood out like a sore thumb. Her mother's quest had always been to get her into a dress, followed closely by her sisters and cousin, who were parroting her mum and her demands for girly attire. Years of inadequacy. Her hair, her clothes,

the way she walked, it was never right.
Stella touched her bare head. She liked the feel of it and the sound it made when she moved her hand back and forth. *Mum wouldn't understand.* It wasn't that Stella didn't want to be a woman, or didn't like men even, it was the narrow definition that she objected to. It felt deeply wounding to her not to be accepted for her choices. She felt sad, thinking about her mother. Even though she pretended that she didn't care about her, she did, really. She wanted things to be different, but her mother was deep into her ways, and she was unlikely going to change. *I might as well follow my own path,* Stella thought. She suddenly felt profoundly tired. She decided to cycle back home carefully. Her ride was smooth. The red lights turned green just as she approached, other cyclists and cars glided by with ease. People were peacefully moving in and out of each other's orbits. One big river, a rhythmical pulse, like the beating heart of this town that deep down Stella did not really hate but was not her home. A city accepting of transitory visitors on their life's journey. When she arrived back at her house, Stella paused for a moment, long enough to notice properly the plaque that was embedded in the cobble stones in front of their building block. A known feature across Berlin, and other cities, it was a Holocaust memorial, that she only paid close attention to now. This one commemorated a Jewish woman, called Hilde, born in 1875. She had lived in their house, was arrested and deported, dying in 1942 in Ravensbrück. Stella bent down, traced the outline of the plaque, and in an involuntary gesture brought her fingers to her lips.
She climbed the four flights of stairs in a pensive mood. They seemed steeper than usual. Later, she looked up Ravensbrück, and found it was a concentration camp for women prisoners, north of Berlin. Jewish women, black

women, Roma women, gay women; taken hostage around the world and imprisoned in the camp. Most were political prisoners, most were killed.

Stella felt a visceral impact of her discovery. She touched her shaved head, *a strange synchronicity*, Stella thought, images of women with enforced shaved heads flashed through her mind's eye. Something inside of Stella coalesced into a burning ball of fire. *These women were murdered. They were denied of their choices. No one can kill me today for making my own choices. Only I can, and I almost did.* The room around her was swirling and the walls were coming down on her. Stella stood there with her arms and hands hanging from her body, now peering at the dark window, as if searching for a sign. All she could see was darkness and her reflection looking back at her. Stella raised her fisted hands up in the air and let out a stifled scream. A big sigh rippled through her chest, and she brought her hands down to frame her face. Suddenly everything made sense. Stella saw her family lined up in front of her. She saw their fear, their oppression, and their hidden fragility. She suddenly understood that she had paid too much attention to their views. That she had let herself be oppressed in turn. *I am free to choose.*

Stella walked over to the radio and switched it on. ANOHNI was singing *Bird Guhl*, and Stella turned the volume up. And as she danced, the sound formed into a wave, flowing through the living room, finding its way into the kitchen and from there into her bedroom. The voice rising to a crescendo, just for Stella, an insistence and assurance, reaching her innermost. Her fragile frame swaying, hands open.

6

Vera
Death

Vera was dying. Most of the people in her life were not ready for her to go, apart from Anna, her housekeeper, and Laura, her great niece, who both knew her well enough to sense her time was counting down. Vera was propped up comfortably in her bed. She and Anna made a good team. Their recent re-organize of her room made sure that everything was within reach from the bed, where Vera spent most of her time now. Her furniture, water carafe, creams, notebook and glasses all arranged in a way to maximize her comfort and most importantly to give her a timeless immersion into her garden, framed by the large windows. The palm trees were swaying gently with a sea of geraniums beneath, their heads zinging in all their colours and glory; deep blood-reds, shocking and soft pinks, crimson, creams and whites. Every morning Anna served her a light breakfast, then helped her wash and get dressed for the day. Anna enjoyed picking out clothes she knew Vera liked and felt comfortable in. She had a good sense for colour. Once Anna was satisfied that Vera had everything she needed, she'd leave her to get on with her day. Vera enjoyed the silence that came after the bustle of the morning routine. She used it to reflect on her life, knowing she had little time left to sort things out in her heart and mind. The view onto the garden, a container that helped her feel focused and at the same time held, the shapes and shades pleasing. Beauty had always been important to her.

Vera had grown up in a little village in the mountainous regions of northern Italy. Perched high on a hill, the village had spectacular views of mountains and valleys all around. It was a luscious landscape where rivers cascaded through the forests gathering into pools, in which they swam as children on hot summer's days. The fresh smell of the water mingled with the musty smell of the earth of the forest was Vera's favourite memory. She enjoyed taking a close-up view of forest life, tracing the furl of the fern, admiring the tiniest moss, looking at the water drops gathered at the ends of leaves, revealing a myriad and mirrored world. The youngest of four, Vera spent a lot of time with her grandmother. They were best friends. Her Nonna was patient with Vera's curiosity, and her slow pace was perfectly suited to Vera's need to stop at every turn. She was kind, patient and deeply connected with the subtle aspect of things, teaching Vera about the plants and their connection to the spirit world.

Their strong bond had given Vera confidence in life, *which has been full of transformations,* Vera thought. *How fortunate I have been and how grateful I am for the gifts that have come my way, starting with Nonna and ending with this paradise on earth.* She had anticipated that one day, this garden of joy would bring her the most profound peace when it was most needed. Vera looked beautiful just like her garden, the cool, peaceful calm of muted colours with splashes of the rainbow of her surroundings playing

with the outside, a dialogue of synergies.
The person who would miss her the most after her death would be her great-niece, Laura. Even though she knew that Laura silently accepted Vera's wish to die. Vera was Laura's surrogate mother and grandmother wrapped in one. Vera's nephew, Carlo met Laura's Irish mother Meg on a pilgrimage to the Vatican. They married shortly after, followed swiftly by Laura' s birth. Tragically, Meg was run over by a lorry after dropping Laura off at day-care, only aged five. Vera never had any children herself but was close to the family, taking an active role in Laura's life after the loss of her mother. Vera was a self-taught sculpturer working with clay, which she introduced Laura to. They spent many a weekend sculpting together. This inspired Laura to study sculpting later one. She had become a fine artist, whose organic wood and stone pieces attracted international collectors.
Laura visited Vera whenever her busy schedule permitted. They enjoyed each other's company, talking all things art, philosophy and spirituality into the early hours. The thought of their companionship coming to an end felt painful in this moment, so Vera pushed these thoughts to one side. Instead, she looked back at her career.
Vera had never been interested in marriage, her busy job in fashion had given her little time to share a life with someone else. However, she had maintained a special relationship with Geronimo, whom she met at her local fruit and vegetable market discussing the merits of eating tomatoes fresh or making them into a sugo. For over forty years, their lives were woven together loosely, both coming and going, depending on the flow of their respective lives. Vera spent many summers with Geronimo who lived by the sea on the Ligurian coast for most of the year. He had inherited a

simple house from his uncle with a small vineyard. Situated halfway down a steep descent to a small unspoilt beach, his place was like a paradise on earth synonymous with his philosophy of life. Life was meant to be enjoyed, and beauty was there to commune with. Close to earth, sea and the sky, his terrace was like an altar, where prayers were said and heard.

His way of being was familiar to Vera from her times spent with her nonna in the mountain forests. Both Geronimo and Vera were good at sitting in silence. They both noticed and enjoyed the simple things in life. Together they bowed to the morning colour palette of blues, azure, turquoise, indigo, and silver giving way to the colours of purple, crimson, coral, bright orange and deep reds at the setting of the sun. It was the place where the goddesses met their male counterparts, where love was the only answer. Vera felt her body ease in the memory of long days and weeks spent together. She had always marvelled at the depth of their bond, which came with a curious absence of a need for possession. When together in that sky and sea hut they were free to love but they were equally free to leave. Vera thought *If I had a wish, it would be one last visit. One last meal together on the terrace watching the sun go down. And when the moon is at its peak Geronimo would dissolve into the night sky. With all my might I would grow wings, shoot up high into the sky and dive sharply down into the water. Down, down I would dive to meet the sea creatures on the sea's bed. And then let death take me.* A sharp pain in her ribs made itself known. Vera had learned much about that pain over the past months, how solitude and her garden made her pain subside, and how frequent streams of visitors and lots of questions increased her pain. Of late, the pain had become frequent and intense, at which point Vera started to ask people to stop visiting and she had started to make plans for the end of her life.

I've had a good life. And I was lucky. Vera thought once more. Her work in the world of fashion meant meeting many frivolous people who provided her with plenty of amusement and meeting a handful of gems whose creativity came directly from the Gods. Vera worked side by side with the creative director of a famous luxury brand. They spoke the same creative language, with Vera assisting him with her affinity with fabrics. Her eye rarely let them down. When he was diagnosed with terminal pancreatic cancer, she was the first to know. He gifted Vera this apartment that became her home, asking her to create a sanctuary of peace, a temple to the arts and creativity. It was something they had often fantasized about. They imagined a place for people to enjoy, to be inspired by, a place that would leave people with more peace in their hearts than when they arrived. The last few years had been the happiest of her life where this vision had become reality. *I am satisfied that I have done all I needed to do,* Vera thought.

She rang her bell to call Anna who swiftly came to her room. "Anna, the wooden box in the back bedroom on the desk by the window, can you bring it to me please?" Anna, who was kind and intelligent, was a soothing presence to Vera. Vera liked her very much and her dedication meant a lot. Anna nodded and within a minute she was back with the box. Vera let her hand glide over the top of it, closing her eyes for a moment as she remembered its origin. Her grandfather had made it for her Nonna many years ago, carved out of pine wood, from the nearby forest.

Vera said "come and sit with me. I am trying to find something for Laura." Vera opened the lid taking out different pieces of jewellery she had collected over the years. She placed them one by one on her quilt, telling Anna the story of each piece. Both Vera and Anna were engrossed like children exploring a treasure chest, handed to them from the bottom of the sea. "There it is" Vera exclaimed happily, finding a piece of jewellery that she had bought for herself on a visit to Sicily. It was a delicate golden necklace with a smooth ruby pendant, encased in an intricate filigree netting. It made a jingling sound when the little ruby ball bounced around in its net. When it caught the light, it came alive, like a little burning ball of fire. Both women gazed at the necklace at the centre of the quilt, absorbed in their own thoughts.

Then Vera turned to Anna with a determined look. "Anna" she said. Anna held her gaze. For a long time, they looked at each other, until both teared up. Vera took Anna's hands in hers. They were warm and soft, strong hands that were confident in what they could do. "You know that I am ready to go" Vera said. Anna nodded. "I've taken care of everything. Tomorrow, I would like you to go the desk in the back room. My will is in the top drawer in an envelope that has your name on it. There are instructions inside. Take the envelope to the lawyer, and she will start the process. Laura is coming this afternoon, and after she leaves, your job will be done. I thank you. You have been an angel, a great help to me towards the end." They embraced each other. Anna framed Vera's face with her hands and said quietly "travel well signora nobile". Anna gathered herself and left the room.

When Laura arrived for her visit that afternoon, the atmosphere was unexpectedly light. Gay laughter rang through the garden and the apartment. The sun came out, and the temperature was pleasant enough for Vera and Laura, arms interlaced, to take a slow stroll in the garden.

Anna brought them afternoon tea with cakes, sandwiches and pastries, which they both liked so much, a nod to Laura's late mum Meg. Laura was delighted with the necklace and expressed her happiness liberally. Vera felt warm inside, her eyes resting lovingly on Laura. Even though Vera kept her plans from Laura, she wanted to spare Laura the exact timing of her death, Vera felt that Laura knew and quietly consented to her plans. To some extent it felt like they were play acting a little, aware that these precious few hours were the last. Laura had known for a while already that she would inherit this apartment, so Vera felt at peace. As Anna was preparing to leave, she met Vera's gaze one last time across the garden. Their eyes said goodbye, and before she turned away, Anna waved one last time. As the sun disappeared behind the high garden wall Laura walked Vera back to her bed. With characteristic vivaciousness Laura started to gather her belongings, stuffing everything into her oversized golden bag, giving Vera a long hug and a noisy kiss on her forehead. "Thank you, Vera. You are the diamond of this world. See you on the other side". They both laughed, and Laura said "joking, see you same time next week".

Alone, Vera leaned back with a sigh and let the echoes of the visit reverberate in the apartment, the sounds slowly giving way to stillness. *Take your time* Vera said to herself, as she sensed an urgency take hold of her *take your time*. She sat there for a good while, watching darkness set in, glimpsing the bats flitting past her windows, back and forth. Vera switched her bedside lamp on, which gave an orange hue to the room, a colour that she had always loved. She leaned over to her bedside table, opened the drawer and pulled out a vial and a small bottle of water. She opened the lid of the vial and then the lid of the bottle and slowly emptied the transparent liquid into the water in the bottle. She replaced the cap and shook the bottle, watching the bubbles settle, which appeared now slightly thicker. She closed her eyes and took a deep breath. Her hands were shaking now, and she was suddenly gripped by fear and doubt. She had anticipated this. She took the crystal carafe that stood on her bedside table for this purpose and poured herself a whisky. She took a big gulp, and she welcomed the burning sensation in her throat. The warmth spread across her chest. Vera was ready to settle into her final project.

She turned her CD player on to play the album she had been listening to on repeat for the past month. This had been a gift from Laura. The album "sleep" by Max Richter, was an eight-hour sound journey, an all-night soother when Vera couldn't sleep due to pain. Increasingly it had become part of her preparation for death. The CD was set to start at Dream 1, Part 5. Vera took little sips of the whisky in time with the music, on every eighth note. She felt steadied. When she sensed that part five was flowing into part six Vera reached over and drank the potion quickly, doubling up with whisky at the end. She felt trepidation but the reassuring taste of the alcohol reminded her of good times relaxing and philosophizing with loved ones, particularly Laura. Part six of *sleep* moved effortlessly into part seven. Faces of loved ones appeared and disappeared in her mind's eye, as if coming to say goodbye. Vera sensed that she was going to drop off soon. She made sure the cap was on the bottle, and placed the whisky glass beside the carafe, neatly. The bats flitted by, perhaps aware of life giving away to death. And when her heart stopped beating, for a moment, everything went exceptionally quiet, as if the world had paused to honour her passing. The sound of a scooter cut through the silence, noisy and insistent. The shouting and laughing

of a couple trailed behind the engine noise, for a moment ringing in the air, the echo of joyful youth and living.
Vera's spirit slowly soared, hovering ever so slightly, between the life of earthly existence, and the journey towards the light. Then it shot off, concluding its transition. Looking from above the scene below was serene. A soft pink light suffused the garden and Vera's room. The green of the palms, in gentle swaying movement, was reaching over the crimsons and rubies of the geraniums, a symphony of strokes and dots. Vera's silent body was held gently by the yielding pillows and the quilt, a still-life of arresting beauty. The colours of Vera's surroundings held everything together, and at the same time streamed towards the beyond. It was a well-composed scene. A car alarm went off, then all went quiet.

7

Darcy

Love

Darcy is stirring.

A shard of light floods through the gap in the curtain into the bedroom and across the foot of the bed where she is sleeping. The former vicarage strikes a solitary and confident figure in this quiet sideroad of bustling East London. Perfectly framed by two London plane trees it stands poised, as if defying the passage of time.

It is Saturday morning, the day after moving and boxes are piled up high. Her identical twin girls, Jada and Grace, just turned three, will soon be awakening to a new day in a new home. Darcy, in her semi slumber, turns over, pulls her eye mask over her eyes and slips back into a comfortable snooze. A thought of her mother crosses her mind, then Darcy remembers the dream. In it she swung her mother onto a white mustang, in one swift and effortless move. She jumped up behind her and together they galloped towards the horizon, a landscape saturated with green. Darcy smiles at her herculean strength in the dream. *I wish* she thought. For a moment she resides in the colour green and fertile landscapes, singing with vibrancy. She has always associated green with her mother, even though her mother disliked all things nature. Lying there Darcy dwells in the atmosphere of the present moment, hovering between what has just passed and what was about to begin, her mother, never far away in her thoughts. Darcy loves her mother deeply, she who is present with unfailing support. Darcy's own quiet support of her mother was to never let go of her mother's story, that still needed telling.

Adopted in the 50s in Liverpool by an elderly Irish couple, who despite their desperation to be parents, were not suited to parenthood, Maureen's life had been lonely and quiet. Her adoptive mother was capable of little affection, and her adoptive father was fearful of the world. They both died within a year of each other when Maureen was only twenty. At first, she felt bereft, but soon felt relief, as the moment of change had arrived. She had always held onto a belief that her sadness surrounding her unknown Irish origins, and her love-less childhood was temporary. She had always felt that love was going to be the driving force of her life, she only had to bide her time.

And so it was, Maureen found love not long after. She met Delroy, a Barbadian, who came with an extended family that kept growing. He was a saxophone player in a successful band at the time, and they had an instant attraction when they were introduced to each other after a gig. Maureen ended up managing their band, finding two families in one go, the music crew and Delroy's big brood. Maureen had always said that Delroy's profound love and respect for her was the beginning of her heart mending, and that her heart was completely mended when she was sat in front of a plate piled high with food from Delroy's larger than life mother. Getting pregnant and Darcy's arrival were the cherries on top of the cake. Darcy loved thinking about those stories

and loved Maureen telling them to her.
Mum's capacity for love has never diminished she thought, *even though she lost the love of her life and became a single mum overnight. Mum is the impersonation of love and has been my guiding light.*
Darcy thinks about her dream again, which reminds her of a recurrent fantasy that she has had about Ireland ever since she was little. Even though Maureen said that she was happy, Darcy always felt that something was missing for her mother. She had always wanted to bring Ireland to Maureen. In this fantasy *Darcy flies above the river Mersey, sweeping along its harbour, taking in the views, following the trajectory of the river until it broadens out into the Irish sea. A pod of dolphins leaps in and out of the water, with Rosie her childhood friend surfing alongside them, waving enthusiastically at her. Darcy drops herself onto a fishing boat where her friend Charlie, a white bearded burly bear awaits with a broad smile. His blue overall matches perfectly the bulging blue hull of the boat, both full-bodied from the years of abundant catches. They sail the Irish sea through stormy weathers and arrive on the island. Rivers and streams gleam from afar in the early morning sun.* Darcy's imagination always fizzles at that point even though she would like her fantasy to find completion with placing her mother in the middle of a big Irish huddle. This morning, she almost manages to complete the image.
Darcy hears the urgent chit chitting of a black bird outside her bedroom window. Then it goes quiet again. She checks the alarm clock and notes that the girls will probably sleep another half hour. She listens into the stillness and saviours its fullness. She stretches her body, then exhales. With gratitude she notes how moving to this new home is

an important milestone for them as a family. She starts to take stock.

Darcy had always known that she wanted to be a mother, but none of her relationships worked out that way. She eventually decided to go solo. She had numerous conversations with several of her gay friends, but no one felt comfortable enough to donate their sperm. She wondered about a sperm bank and briefly contemplated then quickly rejected the idea of getting pregnant in a one-night stand. She thought about freezing her eggs to bide time, but the image of frozen eggs in a container gave her the chills. None of these options seemed right. Then a friend introduced her to the idea of adoption. When she told her mum about it, Maureen went quiet for a few days, saying that she needed time to process a few things. When she came back to her, she said "Darcy, go ahead, I'll be there to help. Your strength and love and kindness will be a million more than what my adoptive parents were able to give me. You will be a great mum".

She remembers the day clearly when the adoption agency rang to say that a young woman pregnant with twin girls with the same mixed heritage as Darcy had just signed the adoption papers. This mother was only seventeen, had no family support, and the father of the babies had left the country with little background information on him. The babies seemed fine, but there were a lot of unknowns. Would she consider?

When Darcy talked to her mother, Maureen was positive. She said, "Having two to love instead of one seems like a gift from the gods. We will deal with the unknowns". In the following days Darcy had felt unusually tired. At the time, her insides seemed to be in movement, and she felt wobbly on her feet. She kept thinking of the sea and how the sensation inside felt like waves trying to break without breaking. She remembers wanting to curl up into a deep sleep and at the same time, she felt she was being pulled backward, as if sucked into a tunnel. Deep down she knew, these sensations signalled that she was making room for new life.

Looking back to that time, Darcy is still amazed how things unfolded. She will always remember the phone call she received to say that the babies had been born prematurely. Her initial reaction had been excitement rather than fear and when they asked if she wanted to visit them, to see how she felt, she immediately said yes. The day of the visit was memorable not just because of meeting the twins for the first time. As she had just arrived in the hospital, there was news that four bombs had exploded on four different public transport sites across London, two not far from the hospital she was at. Darcy remembers hurrying to the baby unit and finding herself sitting between the babies' incubators, feeling jittery and shaky. Absorbing the news in an unfamiliar environment added an uncanny rawness to her fear, that gave rise to doubts about the adoption. She remembers how disorientated she was and how overwhelming everything felt. She remembers one nurse saying to another "this is a protected space, let's keep the news out as much as we can". Grateful for the gatekeeping, Darcy became present to the babies. She remembers looking at the girls, really looking at them. One of them was much bigger than the other, both had tubes going into their noses. The smaller one was twitching and was making peculiar noises. To her they looked like kittens and that thought made her feel more at ease. Darcy remembers getting a strong feeling that sitting there between them quietly was just what was needed for the three of them.

What happened next Darcy remembers with awe. She had felt a pulling sensation between her eyes. A softly rotating yellow globe emerged in her mind's eye, pulsating slowly. A calm and steady energy started to spread across her body. Then the yellow globe began to grow, enveloping the girls in the incubator, the unit, then hospital, then London and beyond. Darcy saw the British Isles from above, including a clear outline of Ireland. She remembers an emergency erupting in the unit, causing a flurry of movement, with several nurses and a doctor attending to a baby at the far end of the room. Darcy tried not to look, and wondered anxiously *what if the girls are sick? Would I cope with health problems*? She had an acute awareness of their fragility and her own vulnerability. Together with the senseless violence of the day's bombing, she felt at the edge. It was the arrival of the nurse that had marked a turning point. She had approached quietly, nodding to Darcy, and briefly checking the girls' charts. She then opened the window to the first incubator and hovered her hand above the baby's tummy, before checking and adjusting the tubes. When she was finished, she gently touched the baby's feet before moving onto the other baby where she did the same routine.

Her approach had felt reassuring, both kind and fair. The nurse had turned to her and said "These girls are special. I have been caring for them since they were born a few days ago. They are strong despite their fragility. I hope they find a good home". She lightly touched both incubators simultaneously and paused for a moment. Then she looked at her and asked, "Are you the social worker?" Darcy shook her head. "You are thinking of adopting them?" She nodded timidly. "Good, you will not regret it". The nurse walked off as quietly as she had arrived. Darcy remembers leaving the

hospital that day determined to take a leap of faith.
In her bedroom, now, in their new home, Darcy revels in the memory of those first days and thinks *the nurse was right; I did not regret it.* She turns on her back, breathing slowly and deeply. She brings her hands up to her chest and feels that warm yellow glow inside. Then she hears a thud coming from next door. *Here they are* she thinks, then she says in a sing song voice "let the day begin".
Darcy jumps out of bed and opens her bedroom door. Jada is lying in the middle of the landing on the sheep skin, she must have dragged from her bed, sucking her thumb and at the same time smiling at Darcy. "Good morning, Jada" Darcy says, as she bends down sweeping her face gently with her hair, a favourite game of theirs. Jada giggles, gets up and grabs her hand pulling her into the girls' bedroom. Grace is still fast asleep, wrapped up tight in her blanket. Darcy pulls the curtains back to reveal a steel-blue sky. Grace stirs, her beautiful round face telling stories of the beyond. Jada taps Grace's chest and says "Wakey Grace. New home time. Wakey!" Darcy sits herself down in the middle of the girls' bedroom, cross-legged among the unpacked boxes. Grace climbs out of her bed straight into her lap. Darcy smiles, feeling yellow and green, warm and settled. She is about to say something when Grace says "Mami, happy". Darcy looks down at Grace who is looking up at her. She frames her face with her hands and says, "Me too Grace, I am happy". Jada was watching them and shouts "Me too, me happy, happy!" whilst bustling into Darcy's lap next to her sister. The three of them wobble and erupt into giggles.
The sound of gurgling rivers over moss-lined rock.
The doorbell rings, and everybody rushes noisily to the door knowing that it is Maureen coming to help unpack. Darcy opens the door and sees Maureen's round face beaming

with anticipation. “Nana!” the girls shout whilst wrapping their arms around her legs, forcing Maureen to steady herself against the doorframe. Maureen laughs loudly. Darcy steps towards her mother, wraps her arms over the girls and around her mother, steadying the whole bundle. They all laugh some more. Maureen then kisses her on the cheek, and says “good morning dear, I am so excited to be here”.

Later in the afternoon, when the girls were settling into their new room, the two women sit down in the kitchen for a break. “Tea mum?” Darcy asks Maureen. Maureen looks at her, tapping the table lightly, seeking her gaze. There is much in those eyes. Recognition. Gratitude. Above all love. Maureen shakes her head slowly, whilst keeping her eyes fixed on Darcy’s. “What?” Darcy exclaims with laugher. Maureen says “Those girls were meant to be here all along, weren’t they? I am proud of you”. Darcy smiles and nods her head. Maureen’s eyes fill with tears. She lightly taps her hand and whispers “happy”. The sun is streaming into the kitchen, spreading a soft orangey light, expanding. *Now let’s have tea.*

8

Sofia
Community

Sofia jumped on her bike.

I need to go to the river or else I'll explode! Sofia's chest felt heavy. Her thoughts were jumbling and tumbling over each other, and her legs felt like they were crawling with ants. It had been a long day of holding things together for other people, of stories piling in. Finally, that part of the day was coming to an end. Earlier, a group of colleagues had come together, the gathering squeezed in between seeing clients and other life commitments. Just a few days ago, Sofia had to break the news of Camila's untimely death. They all knew Camila in different professional capacities in their shared therapeutic community, and they all agreed that she had been a strong character of great importance to them all in their own ways.

Today they had tried to make sense of what could not be made sense of. The news of her death, so unexpected, had been a shock. Made worse by the fact that there was little information on what had happened, nor would they find out since none of them were close enough to Camila's private life to be told. A strange contradiction in the therapy world where intimate connecting sat side by side with unknowing of the personal.

Cycling through the back streets Sofia came to the high street at the end of market day. An assortment of vegetables and fruit boxes were strewn across the street, echoes of busy sales. There was a commotion by the theatre where an alcohol fuelled group of men were shouting at each other, their dogs joining in with excited barking, while a group of people from the theatre were loading heavy equipment, the crates making loud scraping noises as they pushed them into the van. The sun was beating down and even though it was late afternoon, the heat was still unbearable.

An explosion of senses, alarm bells of overstimulation ringing. Sofia took a sharp left away from the chaos, avoiding children, restaurant tables, dogs, and waiters, trying not to breathe in the smells of the fast-food vans, passed the station that spewed out commuters, back onto the main road. Negotiating wild drivers, people criss-crossing, in and out of shops, in this part of the town, Lagos in the making. As she arrived at the end of the high street, she took a sigh of relief. Almost there. It was as if the smell of the river was reaching towards her. She could feel its pull and was impatient to join its generosity.

First, I need a snack. She locked her bike and entered her usual corner shop with its familiar strangers. The Romanian builders, the full body tattooed gentle giant from the barbers across the road, a young woman with a bunch of kids looking for ice-cream, debating which one was best and whether their money would stretch. The Syrian shopkeeper, beautiful, in and out, was serving the whole load with heartfelt dedication "How are you boss? Yes darling! Here you go darling, see you tomorrow darling, ok?! Have a good evening!" His hands busy at the service of multiple realities.

Clutching her locally brewed bear and plantain crisps she left the shop. Just as she unlocked her bike the Vietnamese grandmother from the shop opposite sat down on a creaky chair on the sidewalk and began to hull a bowl of something. Sofia stopped to take in the scene, a momentary still life. The old woman was chewing on something, wholly absorbed in the repetitive task. A sharp noise interrupted the scene and both Sofia and the old woman looked up startled. Their eyes met, and the grandmother broke into a toothless laugh. Sofia chortled along.

Once back on her bike and the busy main road crossed, she relaxed. She was now entering the quieter part of the neighbourhood leading directly to the river. She cruised along the residential road, past the fancy new restaurant that was tucked in between council houses, and further down past the pub that was oozing with booze from behind the stacked-up kegs of beer. As soon as Sofia's bike hit the cobbled path, she got off and excitedly peeled her eyes on the gate at the far end that was leading directly to the water. She pushed her bike with vigour, through that tight passage that was alive with an atmosphere of a time long gone, when ships were built in the yard, with the rich walking alongside the poor, not unlike today, jostling for space and survival. Sofia locked her bike to a nearby railing, then stood at the top of the stairs leading down to the river, with the water lapping onto the steps. The river was still quite full. She loved the river best at low tide, when the beach was exposed for walks and treasure hunts. She checked the tidal times online; low tide would be in a couple of hours. *Good* she thought, *enough time for me to hang around.* Sofia looked for a quiet spot to sit. There was a group of youngsters playing music, laughing, and drinking. There was a stressed looking Chinese man talking on the phone, pacing up and down the promenade. She imagined that he was sad about the closing of the Chinese cultural centre just behind him, arranging for a shipping of the big ornamental chests she admired each time, loading them directly onto a ship from the disused wharf.

Eager to get away from people, Sofia walked to the far end of the promenade. She climbed the railway sleeper wall just above the sign that said *do not climb*. Edging a little to the left she was now behind some big planter boxes with bamboo and seagrass. Hidden from everybody's view she was now positioned perfectly by the river wall that served as handy ledge for her drink and snack. The river was spreading out in front of her. She sat down, opened her can of beer and cheered to the Thames.

Looking out onto the water, she relaxed a little, then noticed the heavy feelings lodged in her body. She wanted to give it over to the river, dirty brown at the edges, a deep blue green further out, swishing against the old wall, breaking, with the spray of water splashing high. Two crows sat perfectly still on the wooden structure jutting out of the river not far from the wall, once used to moor smaller boats. That stillness juxtaposed with the violent flap of the water, reached Sofia's grief and her tension untangled. She let herself cry. *How is it possible that he is dead? Only last week he was alive, emailing me a new date for our next meeting?* A sound came from Sofia's throat, sharp and pinched. As if in response, the crows took off, startled by a big boat speeding by like a rocket. She followed the crow's flight, watching the clouds opening for the sun, revealing a glistening pattern on the water. She was grateful for the release. Sitting by the river, the continuous flow and movement of the water, the views of both stillness and motion, were steadying.

There was still so much to say. The fact I wanted to stop

our collaboration, her attention too often distracted, our words slightly missing each other, not finding a meeting place with ease. We would have talked it all through, ended on a good note... Then Sofia thought *our ending has been robbed by her death.* She remembered her unfailing support of her, her elbowing in for her, teaching her to elbow out when necessary. And yet, something had changed. *Did she know that she was dying and didn't tell anyone?*

Sofia started to rummage in her rucksack, looking for her diary. She got impatient when she didn't find it immediately, tipping everything onto the little pebbled strip in front of the wall. Lip balm, lip stick, her frayed purse, half open, scraps of paper and receipts, an acorn, a little round tin, empty, the echoes of the beeswax ointment, irreplaceable. She held the tin in her hand, turned it to inspect it from all sides, opened it to sniff its faint scent.

She put everything back in the rucksack apart from her diary. On the day she died, she had made a drawing in her diary that took up half the page. The drawing was of the infinity symbol, a figure eight on its side, which she had traced several times with the colour blue. This figure eight was set within a circle, which was coloured in yellow. This in turn was set inside a triangle that she had coloured in green. She looked at it for a while; it looked slightly menacing with the figure eight looking like eyes. She tried to work out if there was any connection to Camila or their relationship, or to death, but none of it made sense. Sofia carefully tore the drawing out of the diary. She found a good-sized stone, which she wrapped the drawing around, snapped off some long seagrass out of the planters behind her to tie up the package. She took a deep breath and with focus launched it as far out onto the water as she could. When it hit the water, the components immediately separated. The stone

sank, the grass floated, and the piece of paper sailed along the ripples of the waves, looking fragile in its exposure to the elements. She watched its trajectory for a while, feeling satisfied that some transformation had taken place.
The tide was slowly receding. Sofia gathered her things and made her way down to the beach. Water was gushing out of an old and broken ceramic canalisation pipe forming channels of water that directed her eyes onto the exposed patches of sand. She started to take photos of the minutiae of collectables; shells, glass, bones, screws, plastics, stones, bricks, ceramic pieces, pieces of clay pipes intersecting with the elements of earth and water, fragments, now smooth, becoming new objects with different meanings.
A young man walked by, avoiding her gaze. Soon he was doing the same as her, keeping his eyes peeled on the beach, occasionally kicking something gently with his feet. As Sofia walked along the river wall her eyes were drawn to something solid. With horror she realised that it was a dead fox. She recoiled a little but then got curious. The fox was dry, untouched by the water, which was strange given that the tide had only just gone back. It must have come down here to die. The eyes of the fox were open, and there were flies hovering over the eyelids. Its hind legs were sprawled wide, as if the fox had collapsed in exhaustion. Its fur was patchy, the bushy tail mangled. Sofia felt as though she had never seen such sadness in a being's eyes, and she was touched by its defencelessness. She tried to imagine what its life would have been like, survival a daily challenge in urban wilderness. She bowed in front of the fox and said out loud *I'm sorry foxy, rest in peace*.
Sofia felt changed by the river's offerings and it was time to leave. She unlocked her bike and thought *if I cycle fast, I can get to the dojo in time*, the space where zen meditation

was taking place. Lev, who Sofia had met only recently, was the monk who was leading the sessions. Today was a special commemorative meditation for those who had passed. She hadn't planned to go, but now it seemed to be the right thing to do.
She arrived at the dojo with just a few minutes to spare. As she entered the building, she was enveloped by the scent of incense, mixed with the soft voices of the people gathered, she felt welcome. As Lev entered, he was surprised to see her. He looked into her eyes, then looked down. A subtle smile crossed his face as he looked into her eyes again. Time stood still, and for a moment it was as if there were just eyes, and it was as though both knew of something deeper. He bowed to her and said "welcome, I am sorry for your loss' and more loudly to the group "let's begin". Someone struck the bell and Sofia settled on the meditation cushion. *Together and alone, alone and together*.

The Sea *is a container. When the river reaches the sea, salty mingles with sweet. The forward motion of the river is subsumed by the unfathomable depth of the ocean. We may never know its vastness, and yet we remember it, because we have come from the sea. Her movement is connected to the rotation of the earth and the gravitational force of the moon. Every day a coming and going. The moon is glowing orange tonight, its face tilted to the side, blowing a good night kiss into the inky blue sky. She thinks 'by the sea I have come to my senses, but more so to my essence'. She inspects the sand from coarse to a fine powder. She watches the water recede, leaving traces, revealing craters and moon landscapes. She zooms in with her imagination; she sees the small as a mirror of the vast. She sits and she knows she is part of this. Parts of her resist. Because it's been a long time. A long time since she was fearless and naked, without doubt. The waves roll towards her and roar. She recognizes the sound. Not just the rage, but pure joy, a thunderous song. Let me be that. Let me be me. Let us be the way we were meant to be. The sea calls.*

9

April
Sea

April was lying on a king size bed with views of the Atlantic Ocean. She stretched her arms and legs out as far as they would go, like a star fish, imagining spanning Ireland from East to West, yawning loudly as she reached the peak of her stretch. She crossed her ankles and placed her hands behind her neck. Looking out of the bay window, her eyes rested on the ash tree, that was framing the ocean, and whose crown was quivering with the glimmer of the morning sun. She was savouring being on her own. Having a double bed to herself with fresh sheets in a new place felt delicious. The silence, and the absence of the other, a deep-felt pleasure. And yet this bed was not hers. Nor was it theirs. Kenji didn't even know of this place, let alone know that she was here away from home. Those last thoughts made her being alone, on this unfamiliar bed, a little less exciting.

What is it exactly I am doing here? April asked herself. Then her thoughts settled on her writing, the stories she had recently picked up again and refined. It felt as though she was at a crossroads, a process that had started fourteen years prior. Seven women had emerged at pace with April's life, the ups and downs of growing her twin daughter, the unpredictability of family life alongside her work as a therapist. April remembers well the day that was the beginning of the women on her pages. That day when the number seven jumped out at her, prompted by her fierce anger towards Kenji leaving them for another business trip. Seven days of being on their own, her seven-year-old twin daughters and her. Looking back, it felt as though April had been holding onto the number seven hard, imbuing it with magical powers, tempering her imploding frustration at the time. A fire she had known needed transforming.

Fourteen years on, April felt different. The sense of sisterhood she had gained from the women that she had written about over the years had settled her anger into something that was more tender and yielding. Her decision to come to Ireland had been somewhat rash. She had needed some time away from the family, and the fantasy that Ireland may hold some key had grown amidst the conflicts they were having. She wanted to understand herself, her mother and her own mothering to her daughters better. Would connecting to this ancestral land reveal something significant? Would she find her mother here? A land she had rejected.

What April really wanted was a sense of homecoming. A homecoming for herself, the daughter in her, for her mother, and somewhere in it all, a homecoming in relation to her daughters. Most of all, April wanted to belong to herself. Her attention turned to her twin daughters. The girls were young women now, having just turned twenty-one. An ache spread across her chest as they appeared to her when they were little. Their chubby faces, their grin, always on the move and busy creating something. She could still conjure up the imprint of their bodies on hers. A soft weight.

Yielding. The two of them warming her body on either side. She missed being their special person. Even though feeding two babies at the same time was a challenge. How impossible it was to keep them all steady. The few times she held them simultaneously precarious balancing acts, their bodies swaying, as if out at sea. The responsibility to keep them safe, frightening in its ultimate illusion. But survive they did, *growth happens no matter what, a belonging together, no matter how*. April still had moments of feeling lost without them, their absence untethering anchors. She wondered how much this had to do with Kenji and their uncertain relationship. All of them waiting. All of them trying to find a new place, a new shape for this family that did not exist anymore.

She got up from the bed and walked over to the window, pausing by the transparent white curtains. She touched the soft fabric, for a moment feeling sheltered in its light protection. Then she pulled them back to reveal the full view that was not familiar, and yet the sea was. The sea had been calling her for a while, the idea of it providing containment for the emptiness, a frequent visitor of late. And yet, being by the sea now, felt unsettling.

She had rented this house, far too big for her alone, because it was beautiful. The large bay windows throughout the house gave way to the elements. The somewhat ramshackle building had a faded beauty, standing confidently, despite its age, at the end of the road, precariously close to the edges of the cliffs that towered above the Atlantic. There was something wild about this location that April, back home, thought would help. A refuge away from the family tensions. Yet on this grey day, April felt suddenly stranded and lost. A few weeks prior, her relationship to Kenji had broken down. Or so she said to herself. The family had spent two weeks together on a holiday in Italy, and it had turned out to be a disaster. As a family they felt disjointed, and as a couple they'd reached a crisis point admitted openly by both, which was a relief after years of silence. The break-down was deeply felt by the girls. April watched them as they both, in their own ways, started working out their alliances and separations within their twinship first, then with their parents, often targeting April over Kenji. Their demand for them to be their still and affixed point seemed entitled and unfair, especially since they were free to come and go. She and Kenji had both resisted those demands, and the tensions created widening gaps between them all. Her and Kenji's union, unlike the girls, had always felt breakable. She often looked at the twins' relationship with awe, watching the ease with which they existed alongside each other, a belonging to each other that was binding them with an invisible thread that could not be broken. Even when they fought fiercely, as they often did. For them as a couple, that unquestionable union was never a given. Fights felt dangerous, the bond at times brittle. Kenji had never felt at home in Europe, as much as he had tried. Looking back now, his constant travels perhaps reflective of a restlessness. Their home in London was ever only going to be temporary. Until the day he announced, matter of fact, 'I have to go home'. April knew that this was a turning point and believed that Kenji, without saying, wanted her to go with him. But that was not what April wanted. Not now. She needed to do something different, for herself, even if she didn't know what that was. Looking back over their almost thirty years relationship, she could see how attracted she had been to Kenji's steady calm. A man of few words. And yet, the precise thing she liked about him then, became the thing she disliked, reading it as an emptiness that she could no longer bear. And yet, it was her own emptiness, not he that was the trouble.

And here she was, looking at the sea.

April thought, *now is about me, giving myself time to create an existence of my own. I don't want to look over my shoulders anymore to check where they are and how they feel and what they need. I just want me to think about. I don't want life to be a constant departure and arrival. I want to feel and grow my own roots.* In contrast to the stories of the women that she had written about, her own story wasn't done yet. Therefore, being here in a new landscape of her own choosing made sense. And yet, April felt a dithering. *This is a bad idea. To come to Ireland, on my own, to find some sort of link or truth, seems absurd now. And silly.* She feared that loneliness was going to swallow her whole.

There was another thing that made April feel ill at ease. A few days ago, she had brought her long and thriving psychotherapy practice to an end. And no one in her family knew about it. She had meticulously planned the closing over months, consulting with colleagues and her supervisor, saying goodbye to all her clients, one by one. She was exhilarated by the task that felt like shedding an old skin. The goodbyes had been bittersweet, as she felt a deep connection to her people and her work. Thinking about it now felt unsettling, with a tinge of guilt. How could she abandon her clients? And yet she knew that she could not put this call for an identity change off any longer. A change that started to have a life force on its own.

Right now, April questioned her wisdom of courting so many endings at the same time. But she couldn't ignore any longer the call to authenticity. The truth was, she did not feel like a mother anymore, not to her daughters, nor her clients, and that called for bold decisions. Not long after their Italy holiday, Aya had decided to visit Kenji in Japan and had no return date planned. This seemed like a clear declaration of solidarity on her part with Kenji. April was afraid of losing Aya, of losing her to Kenji whose calm aligned much more with Aya's needs. Sora who was now called Ray, was madly in love with another girl. She was intensely attached to Ray, which made April uneasy. April sensed a bewilderment in Ray similar to hers, as if she was searching for a replacement for what she had lost, both the relationship to her twin sister as well as her parents.

A change in the weather drew April's attention to the sheets of grey clouds that were moving rapidly from east to west. A flock of birds almost lost control in a gust of wind. *We are all lost in our own ways, lost to each other,* April thought, as she was watching the birds regain control and scoop down towards the beach and out of her sight. *Except for Kenji perhaps. He is back in his homeland, with Aya his ally by his side, the two of them satisfied with each other's company, unconcerned with what they have left behind.* For a split second she felt her old hot anger rising, visualizing smashing the window with her fists, imagining the pain of splintered glass and blood spilling. The image gave way to conciliatory thoughts.

Perhaps this isn't quite true. Kenji and Aya just don't do guilt in the same way I do, and Sora aka Ray is equally haunted by bouts of guilt. This made April think of their oppressive catholic heritage, passed down from the long line of Irish mothers and daughters. *Kenji's ways are different,* April thought. *He does not seem to bend under pressure, from outside or inside. He goes along with life as it presents itself to him from day to day.* Perhaps that's what April found difficult to handle over the years, taming her raging guilt and shame under the gaze of Kenji's steady way of being. *Kenji going home was an authentic act of responding to his heart's need*, April thought. A sudden yearning for his arms raced through her. April had to steady herself against the windowsill. Rain was now crashing against the panes. April took a step back. *I don't know where or what home is.* And that last thought made her crawl back into bed. Under the covers, she thought about how restless and busy she had been all her adult life, how rarely she had allowed herself to rest. *Busy with life and parenting*, April thought, *busy keeping dark thoughts at bay*. She wrapped herself up and fell asleep. Her sleep brought her a dream.

> *April found herself looking down onto the world. Earth was moving and turning slowly in 3D, enveloped in a peaceful atmosphere. It was floating in arcane blue; ocean, night sky and galaxy combined. A network of light began to grow over the world like a cloak, as if knitted by invisible hands. Hundreds of globes holding together the connection points of the net, sparkling points of shining light. There was a silent quality that seemed to be beckoning.*

April woke with a startle. She sat up, leaning against the headboard, marvelling at the vivacity of the images. She noticed her hands resting on the white sheets, taking note of the wrinkles and creases. Some time passed. April felt calm. She got up to look at the sea again and the weather had calmed too. She opened the windows, tasting the salty air, which felt inviting. There and then she made a renewed commitment to her project of being here in Ireland, on her own, despite the uncertainty.

The next few days were filled with a serenity that felt new to April. Her daily routines had a good pace and brought her pleasure. Each morning, she made a small loaf of soda bread and then took herself for a brisk walk on the beach. She made a daily pilgrimage to the local tabletop mountain exploring its many pathways. Sometimes she found the mountain bleak, at other times she was taken by its honest beauty. Curiously, she never made it to the top, even though that had always been her plan. Instead, she let her imagination complete the story of being at the top. There, she was looking over the Atlantic Ocean across to America, with a vision that stretched to its shores. Simultaneously her vision of the world suffused by the net of light appeared in her mind's eye. In her imagination she was fusing the image of her standing on the mountain top with the twinkling net of lights, thinking *somewhere beneath all of that is me, working out my life.*

She dipped in and out of the image of the network of light as she went about her days. She started to explore the surrounding area in her rental car going further afield, using the sea as her reference point. Trying to keep the trinity of mountain, land and the sea within reach of her eyes. She visited Coney Island *oh like New York's Coney Island* April thought with delight, that could be reached at low tide only, which was an exciting adventure. As she was jogging along the sandy beach to warm up after a short dip in the icy water, a thought, like a possibility, started to take shape in her mind. *What if I take sail from Ireland to America, a straight-line due West. And Kenji at the same time takes sail from Japan to America, a straight-line due East. At least, straight enough. I land on the East Coast, and he lands on the West Coast. Then we can meet somewhere in the middle.*

She felt a little childish entertaining such fanciful imaginings, but the thought persisted. Over the course of the next few days, it took on various forms. Sometimes she rode on the back of a whale rather than a ship and Kenji was part of a pod of dolphins. Other times she superimposed her 3D 360 degree spinning world onto their respective journeys, with the net of light as a guiding beacon.

April was surprised that America had entered her mind. America had always been off the cards, an active rejection of her father and his homeland. After all, he was born in the deep south, in the shadows of oppression, a domination that continued with destructive industrial practices that polluted its many bodies of water. She decided she needed a physical map to get a sense of her internal geographical visualisations. She visited different charity shops in search, and eventually found one, old and half torn. The shopkeeper kindly said she could have it for free, since she had also bought a biker jacket and some leather boots that were as good as new. She was still intending to climb that mountain. Happily, she hurried back to the house, feeling her creative energy building.

It was early afternoon, the light and the wind felt gentle and warming. It was a week into April's stay, and it felt as though she had always been living here.

April put her new boots on, as well as the leather jacket, and stomped around the house with all windows wide open. She enjoyed the sound the boots made on the wooden floorboards with the wind blowing through the space. She poured herself a glass of whisky, pushed the round dining table close to the window and spread the map out. Marvelling at the amount of water on Planet Earth, she noted how dense and locked-in Europe was. Fascinated by the various cargo routes, she tracked travel times from

Asian locations to European ports, using a shipping app on her phone, drawing the routes with a black pen. She appreciated the strategic construction of the Suez Canal, and the importance of the strait of Gibraltar, both crucial slip throughs to get to the British Isles faster, docking at Southampton port, Britain's trading gateway to the world. Scanning back to London, April looked for Tilbury docks on the North shore of the river Thames, imagining the arrival of the Windrush, bringing the first post-war migrants to Britain from the Caribbean. *Arrival of people and goods breathing fresh air into old stuffiness, ships bringing new flavours, world connections and geopolitical tussles* April thought. She imagined herself on board a cargo ship. What might that be like, with just water, birds, sky, and sea-life for company?

The journey would be easier if I was a fish, April thought, the image reminding her of Paul Klee's fish in his Notebook. The fish that had continued to live inside of her all these years, symbolizing freedom and change. Then she remembered the sail of the ship she had spotted on the river Thames, seen from her library window seat, pairing the two images, fish and sail, once more in her mind, an auspicious collage. With her black pen, April sketched one round fish off the coast of West of Ireland, and another long fish at the other side of the world off the East Coast of Japan. She imagined hopping onto the whale's back to go and visit Kenji in Osaka. But as the whale approached Osaka Bay, it refused to deliver her to the shore. Instead, it turned around and swam back into the vastness of the Philippine Sea, hovering at the edges of the North Pacific Ocean. *Why would you not deliver me old whale*? April asked. She wanted to tell Kenji about the map and the shipping routes, finding herself talking to him quite a bit.

She thought about how her anger, or rejection of Kenji was her hatred for her father, and ultimately a deep buried hate mingled with shame towards herself for her vulnerability, her need for love and support that did not reach her as a child. April had never liked feeling vulnerable.
April moved to the window with a second glass of whisky to watch the sunset play with the surface of the water. The sea was spectacularly wild, and the beauty made her well up. April returned to the map. Leaning onto the table she looked at it, wondering *will I find a home, me, with this map? Could the map hold the solution to my question of should we or should we not separate?* Pursuing her thoughts despite herself, April located Los Angeles as Kenji's arrival port, and New York as hers. She poured over the map to find an obvious approximate middle place for them to meet. She drew an imaginary line between the two cities, and her eyes set on Oklahoma. Oklahoma was Indian territory, so much she remembered. It had ancient mountain ranges, prairies, and mesas, which were vast expanses of tabletop mountains, *the bigger versions of the local tabletop mountain I have tried and failed to climb* April thought. At the thought of the expansiveness of that imagined landscape April morphed into an eagle flying high above, looking down, owning the vastness of its freedom. She started to feel a little queasy, perhaps the second glass of whisky had not been a good idea. Thinking about America took her too close to her paternal heritage. She really had a profound dislike of her father's ways and what he represented. Despite her reservations, she felt like she was getting pulled into something she could not stop. She looked up how far Birmingham, Alabama, was from Oklahoma. *Perhaps we can go on a road trip and see where father grew up.* She conceded, *not all of father is bad and*

there are some good memories. He took her fishing when she was little, and he always spoke with fondness about his own mother who died early from a bone disease. She was half Cherokee. April remembered an old wall hanging in her father's study in their last family home, a family heirloom, with a river and fish motif stitched on a red background.

That night April fell into a deep and dreamless sleep. The next morning Sora aka Ray, called her. She could tell that she was suspecting something. She kept asking her "is everything ok Mum?" "Yes, all is well". "How is work going?" A question she dodged successfully, April thought. As for Kenji and Aya, they hadn't been in touch, which was all for the better. Whatever everyone was doing or feeling, it didn't hold such pressing importance for April anymore, which felt liberating. Since finding the map, April had found herself. She felt connected in a way she hadn't for a long while. Her days spent at the dining table overlooking the sea had entered a timeless dimension. Old rights and wrongs had disappeared. She found herself in a cycle of thinking, researching, writing, and thinking some more. She had found the gate to her dreamtime. And with that, her desire to climb the mountain, and understand all things ancestry had disappeared. In the evenings, April started to sit on the bench in front of the house, wrapped in a woollen blanket, in a sort of meditative state. Sometimes even snoozing a little. She felt no urgency, no fear. The answer to all her questions seemed to sit in the in-between of the elements; earth, water and sky.

April treated herself to a complete second-hand set of Paul Klee's notebooks, something she had wanted to do for a long time but never dared. The books arrived a few days later, delivered by a cheerful postman whose singing could be heard well before he arrived at the door. April found herself humming along. She placed the two heavy notebooks on the table, side by side and opened each book to find a pleasing page, that reflected her process. Perhaps the ending of the mothering cycle; attending to others, facilitating a meeting place in a field where both darkness and lightness could meet. Both for her daughters, and for her and Kenji's relationship. As April looked at Klee's shapes, circles and dots, his annotations and numbers, his pacing and his command of a line and a curve, she felt a renewed joy of art in its purest form, art in all that the eye could see, in all that the heart could hold.

Then April remembered her angel visions from her childhood, which had rested forgotten in her memory.

Out of the blue, she felt a tingle, and a little pause in time and space. She heard a voice call her that came with a brief vision of an old woman with rugged skin and long braided hair. She had a sensation of someone gently shaking her shoulders. A warm current ran down her spine. April now remembered; her visions of angels had stopped when her period had arrived, and the angels had never returned. April had never even questioned the fact. It was as if the arrival of the blood, of womanhood, had stripped her of this celestial connection, and wiped her memory clean.

April counted, she had bled for 40 years, that cycle now completed in her menopause. Her period had arrived late when she was 15. April noted that her visions of angels had lasted for seven years. Here was that number again.

The arrival of her period had been deeply troubling to her teenage self. It had gushed out of her thick and fast, leaving her shocked and disgusted. She had refused to go to school for a whole week, crying every day. She felt so miserable that she was sure the only way out would be to end her life. She remembered her mother handing over some pads,

saying matter of fact "welcome to the sisterhood dear, you'll get used to it".
Interestingly, her mother did not mind her being off school, nor did she object to her crisis, which was unusual, as her mother had never tolerated a break in routine or tears. This was the most supportive her mother had ever been. Occasionally she had come into her room, had patted her back, and had said "this too shall pass". April was surprised by these emergent memories. She felt warm inside, and she registered the presence of her mother and an absence of anger. In her mind's eye she saw her father stand next to her mother, smiling and holding up a fish.
The next day April received a message from Kenji. He'd sent her a selfie of him and Aya, both looking happy. Kenji's text said, "curating opportunity in the US". She felt a jolt in the pit of her stomach and texted back saying "meet in the middle?" He replied with the thumps-up emoji. Then a text arrived from Sora aka Ray saying "Mum, I'm single again, it's for the best" signed Sora. A second text followed shortly after, saying "I'm off to join dad and Aya for a quick visit!"
None of this makes sense, April thought, *and yet all makes sense. Ray is back to being Sora, who is joining Aya, Beautiful Sky re-united. And Kenji? It feels as if he has been part of my thoughts and here with me all along*. April looked out of the window at the sea. *America, really*? Her heart skipped a beat.
April caught a glimpse of her map on the table, and for a split second it seemed as if it was taking off, fluttering like a bird. Wrapped in the network of light, a mist was lifting, revealing rivers, interspersed by lakes, amidst the vastness of the ocean. April shook her head and smiled. Her eyes skimmed from east to west on the map, settling on North America. Images of giant trees, fast moving water and

swaying grass, were running across her mind's eye like a film. *Rivers always flow into the ocean*, April thought. *There is no other way, the untangling takes place no matter what.* April grabbed a blanket and sat in front of the house just in time to see the sun drop into the sea. For a split-second April thought she caught a glimpse of her pink hued angel courting the sun. From the urban landscape of her childhood, her angel looked at home in the seascape of her ancestral homeland. April's heart skipped another beat, and a thousand butterflies released into her stomach. Then stillness. *Mum was right*, April thought, *this too shall pass, this long long torment of questions about me and Kenji, about life, about who I am, this too shall pass.*

It was as if something heavy was lifting, dissolving into the receding crimson strip on the horizon, one heartbeat at a time.

Part II

10

My Mother

It all began a year before my mother's death. During an Easter holiday when my children were small, we went to the Maritime Museum, which is just a few minutes away from the river Thames. My daughters and I took part in a community creative event, while my son was napping in the pram. It was a struggle to get him to sleep, but I insisted, as I sensed it was important for us females to have protected time. The hall where the workshop took place was bright and inviting. An assortment of small objects, fabrics and colourful paper were scattered across different tables. The theme of the event was 'remembering those who passed' with the invitation to create something representative. The workshop organizers had created makeshift shelves from the available material for display of the finished pieces. There was a happy atmosphere in the air, and the event felt generous and celebratory. Since we didn't know anyone who had passed, I suggested that we create something to celebrate my mother, their grandma. We decided that my mother loved reading, sewing and swimming, which she had passed down to me, and I had passed down to the girls. I chose swimming. With thick blue paper, I fashioned a swimming pool and made a stick figure to represent my mother. I then scrunched up some golden wiring into a ball that I placed in front of her. I imagined my mother chasing the golden ball as she swam up and down the pool. My memory of that day is one of ease and flow. We proudly displayed our works on the shelves and took photos. The next day I told my mother about our creations. She laughed and said, 'why would you choose to celebrate me when I am not dead?"

A month later my mother got diagnosed with pancreatic cancer. Ten months later she was dead.

*

My mother's death was heartbreaking, and it was also liberating. My mother's death meant my birth. Just as my mother gave birth to my body at the beginning of my life, she made space for my spiritual self in my mid-life when she passed over to the spirit world. Before her death I was bound to her. Her unhappiness was tied to my happiness and diminished it in the process. I was indebted to her for the sacrifices she made. With her death my debt was cleared. When I saw my mother's dead body, I had a strong sense that she had departed from earthly existence in a shot. From then on, she seemed to tell me that I owed everything to myself, and myself only.

My mother did not reveal much about her inner life and rarely talked about her feelings. This was difficult for me. I had a need for her revelations, so that I would be able to reveal myself in turn, to myself, her, and the world, as a girl, as a woman. Instead, I learned to keep my inner world to myself, just as she did. Her unknown internal life felt like a dark abyss to me, threatening in its emptiness, whereas my inner world felt filled with light. I didn't always know what to do with that. I was confused by the difference.

My mother is the most important person in the world. I spent a lot of time rejecting that. She lives inside of me as a daily point of reference, where lines are drawn and re-drawn. She housed me inside her body and then she gave birth to me. I know that my mother breastfed me for three months and enjoyed the stillness of the night. This is a precious piece of information, as it gives me hope that she enjoyed me.

Following male medical advice my mother stopped breastfeeding me at three months. I was told that I cried every night for three years.

I often get trapped in causal thinking when I think about my mother. I am like this, because she was. In truth, my mother and my feelings about her are complex. There are many facets to my mother.

I recently found black and white photo-booth pictures of her. Two out of the four photos are missing, perhaps she needed them for a new passport. The two remaining photos show a playful side to her, in one she looks up into the sky, in the other she throws a confident side gaze to the camera. She looks beautiful.

There was a time when I was filled with painful yearning for her when confronted with her beauty. Today I feel curious.

Migration is at the heart of my family's story and evokes complex feelings. Choice sits alongside yearning and questions of belonging. Distance between one significant place and another is a constant reality that needs navigating. Internal representations of the meaning of those places shift, whereas the practical givens of travelling don't. My mother was pushed to migrate from England to Switzerland in the 60s, and I was pulled to do the reverse journey years later, compelled to live a different life from the one given to me, which my mother may have felt about her migration too.

The phone was central to our daughter and mother relationship. The landline was a solid object representing the somewhat incomprehensible fact that news can travel in cables across bodies of water and land, the invisible cords becoming meaningful, often emotional messengers. I grew up watching my mother countless times talk to her sisters on the phone, always sitting in the same armchair by the window, where tears and laughter where interchangeable, irrespective whether it was happy or bad news. They were good at dark humour. I phoned her with news of pregnancies and pregnancy losses, which would have evoked in her conversations about joys and sorrows from across the water. Learning about significant life events from a distance had always carried a particular heaviness and sadness for my mother. My mother never stopped being homesick.

The distance meant that we experienced poignant moments that might not have happened in person. Occasionally my mother drew a line and would say "this is not a conversation to be had over the phone". When 9/11 unfolded my mother and I were on the phone with each other witnessing simultaneously the collapse of the second tower on our respective TV screens. Her stifled cries are still vivid in my memory.

Towards the end of her life, I made it a habit to ring her after school drop offs. Standing by our front windows with a generous view onto the world, these are the conversations I miss the most. They were light and gentle, where we both drew comfort from sharing the familiar of the everyday that was mothering and domesticity. That ease was never replicated when we spent time in person. Closer to her death my mother called me one morning, asking me "Why am I in so much pain"? It's probably the only conversation I had with her where I stepped into the role of the therapist. I sensed it was emotional pain she was experiencing, and I talked about how emotional pain can be felt physically and that this pain may well be linked to her life story. I didn't ask her any direct questions about that pain. That would have been out of character for our relationship. Today I would be able to ask, but not then.

In our last telephone conversation, I had said my final goodbye to her in person a few weeks earlier, I told her that I was thinking about coming to see her again. She said, "don't come, we will meet in the sky". At the last hour I decided to go anyway, listening to an urgency I felt inside. The process of making that decision had been agonizing and had resulted in me double booking my flights. I wondered why say another goodbye? Did I want to be there when she took her last breath? Did she even want me there? I didn't have an answer. All I knew was that I had to go to honour the transitional space between life and death.

In the last few telephone conversations my mother's voice had changed; her musings took on an otherworldly quality. When her stomach was bloated from the spread of the cancer, she joked that she looked like she was pregnant with twins. When I asked her whether she was expecting boys, she vehemently said "no! it's girls, always is and always will be girls". I was struck by this outcry in her last hours, as she had always appeared more comfortable with boys.

*

My last journey to see my mother was a mid-morning flight on an Easter Sunday. Before leaving I had the urge to arrange the breakfast table for the family, a last precious communal meal that was a precursor to a fundamental change. As I left the house, I had to force myself to walk and not look back. My feet felt like they were wading through treacle. A certainty had settled inside of me that I was never going to see my family again. It's a feeling that still echoes to this day when I leave the family home to travel on my own.

I was nervous when I boarded the aircraft. My seat was in a row of three that I shared with two young men. I remember being struck by their presence. Both were in their thirties, of Asian descent, calm, courteous and attentive to me joining their row. They were also both strikingly handsome. Once we were settled in our seats, they both took out their laptops. One of them was working with complicated formulas, the other was working on something creative. As soon as we took off, the aeroplane was caught in a violent turbulence seemingly coming out of nowhere. The plane shook from side to side with loud bumping noises. I can't recall the men next to me reacting to this at all. I on the other hand was gripped by terror, sure that we were going to crash. I debated with myself for a moment how I felt about dying and then decided, if that was the case, so be it. The moment I let go of my fear the aeroplane pushed through the clouds, and we were flooded with light. All was still, and I fell asleep.

When I arrived on the other side, I was greeted by my brother with the news that my mother had died. When I rang home, my husband told me in distress that our daughter had fainted inexplicably in the park while roller-skating. We double-checked the times of my mother's death, my experience on the plane and my daughter's fainting. The times coincided. At the time of her passing, my mother, my daughter and I had 'joined in the sky'.

In the Easter holiday of one year, my daughters and I celebrated my mother (and her impending death) with art, on Easter Sunday the following year my mother died. A few months later, I a miscarried a foetus whose due date would have been the Easter of the following year. A three-year creative arch of transformations during the festival of re-birth.

11

My Self

When I think of myself and my life, it is almost impossible to think of a coherent Self. And yet, I sometimes sense my Self as an entity that has a reality and meaning that goes beyond the nitty gritty of the everyday. I can feel whole, in one piece and together, moving along in a flow that feels generous. When I breathe, and I am in touch with earth, my Self becomes a field where the stories of my life converge into an expansive whole. There are times when I feel fragmented and lost, searching for something familiar, entangled in doubts and fragments of living. In that instance, the body and landscapes of my being consist of multiple stories clashing. My Self is coherent and incoherent. The art of living is finding, losing and re-establishing balance between coherence and incoherence. My body is the vehicle that contains all my being, both internal and external sensations, subjectivities and objectifications of my existence. When I manage to inhabit my body and breath with ease and flow, I am Self. In my day to day, inevitably I engage in the activity of trying to make sense.

Making sense of my life is making sense of my experiences, my life as a woman, mother and therapist.

Sense-making as a *woman* is noticing my bodily changes

over time. Learning to step into a body that is just mine. Now, a body too old to create another human, with a springiness that feels different to when I was in the throes of motherhood.

Sense-making as a *mother* is to sit with the mystery of growing children inside of me, coming to terms with attachment and letting go, at birth and at every point of developmental change.

Sense-making as a *therapist* is to be with another human being, and to be brave in the face of the unknown, both theirs and mine, that sometimes transforms into something we call a truth, for now. Courage is needed in the face of our worlds colliding.

Life asks me to let go every day, with questions about emptiness and fullness. The task of finding a way in life and in relationships, as a mother, woman, and therapist edges up to the question of what is human? How to be human?

Woman, mother, therapist are not just roles; they are ongoing experiences of being human.

Making art and creativity help me process my being human. The act of making sense through creating collages and still-lives of feelings, experiences, events, questions and uncertainties facilitates transformation.

When deaths were colliding, I adorned sticks with wool and feathers and bells. I gave one to my friend after she gave birth to her dead baby boy. I made one to symbolize my mother's passing. I made one to stoke the fire at every full moon for a whole year. I made another one to practice letting go, and to remind myself of the endurance of my bond to my children, no matter what. The act of creating helps me out of the dark places where I got lost, finding my way back into the light.

I sense myself to be separate and at the same time I am

connected; to people, places, memories, hopes, and desires. I am my feelings, my perceptions, my thoughts, my recollections, my relationships, and my fears. My senses of myself and my body are mine, yet they do not belong to me entirely, because the world has already made an image of me before I was born.

Because of that I notice a battle in me. My thinking and my language are affected by social conventions, sneakily, and imposingly. There is a type of linear thinking inside of me that is pushy and tries to assert its truth, it loves its normative ways. It demands for evidence, for explanation, for solutions that fix problems. It's an unkind presence that entangles me.

I was taught to pay attention to the words that come out of me and to make sure that they appease and adapt. A restraint that throws a veil over my truth.

I hide my random thinking, and my incoherent experiences inside of me, for fear of being ridiculed, dismissed or shut down. There are right and wrong ways of doing things, I hear a voice whisper.

Sense making through art and creativity is a rebellion against patriarchy.

I want to engage in active resistance.

I as a woman, as a mother, and a therapist must actively resist that which is imposing. I do not want to tread a line that was given to me.

I choose, and I create. My world is round. In that circle all and everything is welcome. Experiences that connect me to other experiences, to other people and places, creating more circles, like ripples in a lake. Experiences that are allowed to be random.

Meaning making. I offer stories that feel true now. Tomorrow those stories will be different. The aim is to offer something

that moves, that is cumulative and transformative.
I am a woman, and I want to celebrate women. Women are mothers to emptiness and fullness.
I want to celebrate life, which is unthinkable without mothers. Mothers don't get celebrated. Women's life experiences are not valued. It is the woman who gives birth to life. We can't understand life without looking at the female experience. We can't honour life without honouring the mother.
The denial of the mother, the female experience, the woman, is femicide. I felt that in my life. I felt it in my mother.
In my dual position as a mother to my daughters and daughter to my mother, I look both ways and I want to create a space where I can thrive, searching for what is possible now that was not possible then. For my daughters, for women. I want to be brave and reclaim my humanity. So that we can be ourselves, uncompromisingly, a human me, unconditionally.
I am of the earth. As a woman, my cycles, my womb, the cyclical nature of my body, the flow and the drying up of my blood feels earthy. The mystery of these processes goes hand in hand with intense sensations and feelings, with an internal life that is rich and does not care about logic. It does not conform to the demands of rationality and functionality of the outer world that prefers it to be forgotten and stay invisible. And yet this internal world is a precious gift to the outer world, offering an atmosphere of being that contains truths about growth and the ebb and flow of life. It knows about patience, endurance and shape shifting.
I imagine the women from my matrilineal group populating my internal earth. A sisterhood united around our shared struggles, our shared wisdom. Women who pass me by in the street, with their own internal earthly seeds, each

woman with an important story to tell. There have been moments in my life where I met women with Irish ancestry, to whom I felt a strong affinity. Like we shared a creative code. Perhaps the cloth of my Irish ancestry is stronger than I know.

*

For many years my focus was on trauma, mine and that of others. There was an ache and a darkness, that I felt was passed down the ancestral line, particularly the female one. When my twin daughters were toddlers, I went to a family constellation workshop where I wanted to experience first-hand the theory that any given field contains information from the past. In this system, the client states what they want to clarify, then they choose from a pool of observers, representatives to stand in for the things or people that belong to the initial question. Representatives are then asked to move or speak as it emerges in that field. It shows how the energetic imprint of a person or situation survives time and space, expressed with incredible accuracy and detail that only the client would know to be true. Often additional information is revealed that helps the client understand more than they did before. I will never forget seeing representatives lying down in a row on the ground embodying the countless miscarriages a woman had, information that had not been revealed to the group but turned out to be true.

For my constellation I wanted to understand more about the silence of my mother. I was initially asked to choose a representative for my mother, for my grandmother and my grandfather. Later in the session a representative for my great-grandmother was brought into the constellation.

This is before I researched my ancestry or knew her name to be Ellen. My mother's representative kept a safe distance from me, which she voiced as being good for her but was painful for me. My grandmother's representative rubbed my cheeks gently, a gesture that was familiar; my mother, aunties and I use it to express love. It was the person representing my great-grandmother Ellen that revealed information that was going to be profound for my journey of discovery of my Self. Ellen was alone and distraught, and she kept saying "there is no support", repeatedly, while her body was doubling over with spasms.

This was astonishing, as I knew this physical movement with the accompanying words well. My body used to double up in spasms when I was distraught with the same words and feeling of no support. I used to call it the black hole. It's an experience I had never understood and felt like a sensation at the edge of death, like falling into a dark abandoned place.

Here was a visceral and energetic link of feeling abandoned with no help, 102 years apart, between me and my great-grandmother Ellen.

*

Years later, amid writing this book, abandonment came up once more. I was drawn to go to a particular place in my local park, that I wouldn't usually go to. When I turned the corner to an area I knew contained flower bedding, I was hit by the intensity of the colour orange radiating from rows and rows of African Marigolds that had been planted. As I absorbed the colour, reminiscent of saffron robes of Buddhist monks, the German name for these plants *Tagetes,* common in my childhood, popped into my head. As soon as I said the plant name my mother appeared. She beamed at me, embraced me and told me she loved me. My chest, then my body, were inundated with a deep warm feeling. I was moved to tears and as quickly as the vision had come, it had disappeared. For weeks after, I only had to say the word *Tagetes* in my mind to bring about the deep warm embrace of maternal love.

When I drop into *Tagetes* now, for a moment my Self feels present, alive and at peace. In that moment my Self is whole and I am.

12

My Ancestors

In search of my mother, I found four generations of my female ancestors. They lived in Newcastle; a stone's throw away from the River Tyne. For about 80 years my female ancestors brought up their families in the same street, occasionally changing house number, in what would have been tightly packed tenement flats, sharing their quarters with numerous other multigenerational families, mainly migrants, many from Ireland. At any given time, it was normal to be part of a household of ten to twelve people. The city, a powerhouse of the industrial revolution, needed willing labourers for the ship building and steel industry. My ancestors were workers and the river with its industry provided a solid source of income.

When I think of my female ancestors, I think water. In my imagination, I see its flow a short walk from their tight living quarters. I see its flow a welcome movement to stifling dark rooms of scarcity. I see its flow a welcome interlude to hardship that I learned was at times unbearable. In the flow of water is where dreams begin, is where hope is born.

It took a while to sift through ancestral information and threading the daughters and mothers together. For a long time, Bridget was the head of my matrilineal group. Only more recently I learned about Cecilia who is now the top mother. She left Ireland in 1851 leaving the Roscommon area, which was one of the hardest hit places in Ireland by the famine. The family that arrived in England was small, leaving me wondering how many had been left behind, how many had starved to death.

Eight generations of women separated by 200 years from the birth of my great-great-great grandmother Cecilia to the birth of my daughters. A flow of sisterhood connecting the now and the past.

Finding my female ancestors has filled my Self, bringing together all coherent and incoherent parts, where all are welcome, where we all belong.

I hold my matrilineal group in my mind and heart, and it looks like this

my twin daughters
they stand side by side
I stand behind them
my mother Margaret stands behind me
my grandmother Margaret stands behind my mother
my great-grandmother Ellen stands behind my grandmother
my great-great-grandmother Bridget stands behind Ellen
my great-great-great-grandmother Cecilia stands behind Bridget

In conversation with my mother's youngest sister, she once said "I can't comprehend how your mother could have moved to Switzerland, a landlocked country. She who loved the sea so much".

There are five bends in the River Tyne from where my ancestors lived before you reach the North Sea and Tynemouth pier, which was a place my mother loved. There is a photo of me and her taken by my father. We are standing on the pier, my mother's eyes are closed, and her body is leaning ever so slightly into mine. We all knew that her death was only months away.

*

It is a cold and sunny winter's morning.
I decide to go on a walk to my local park to visit the trees. I haven't done this for a while, and with gratitude I inhale the crisp air. I am excited in anticipation of being with the trees. Over the years I've had experiences with Cedar, Beech, Elder, Apple, Laurel, Maple, Plum, Willow, Dawn Redwood, Yew and Pine trees. Cedar has become my go to tree, generous in her guidance, as I frequently sit under her canopy. I have learnt to ask questions and listen to the messages that the trees transmit. It's a process of dropping into my body and wait long enough to receive something that is helpful. And it always is.
As I am walking along, this sentence drops into my mind.

The end of being the mother as the central figure
(is not the end of mothering)

I know that I have been grieving for the past few weeks. My grief is multidimensional. It's the loss of my daughters who have gone to study in two different places, it's the loss of their twinship as we knew it, it's the loss of my fertile years, it is the loss of my mother and what she represents. All wrapped in one.
I haven't wanted to acknowledge the grief, but my aching back is telling a different story. My body is tense and is struggling to unfurl. My pain started on the left side of my lower back, and after some osteopathic treatment it

has moved onto the right. I keep moving in a way I know loosens these tensions, but as soon as I get on with the day the tension snaps back. My body is asking me to listen to my grief. I am listening, in a way, but at the same time I am not.

I take stock. I reflect that I have been good at finding medicine for my healing over the years. I am good at self-care, so I say to myself. Even so, there is a kernel of pain that I am pushing away.

I enter the park. The first trees on my walk are the willows that I associate with grief. One of the willows is old and I imagine she is the mother of the two younger ones opposite. Her knotty trunk is about five times my size. I touch the trunk gently, then lean on it. I say hello and ask for guidance. "What is it with my grief? What is it I am needing to understand?" The willow gives me an image; a river flowing into the ocean. I say to the willow "I am scared of the transition from the river to the sea". The willow does not provide me with any more guidance but gives me a memory instead:

It's the summer of the year my mother told us about her cancer diagnosis. We are on holiday by the coast on the English Channel. We find ourselves at the mouth of a river that is so full it tears wildly into the sea. A strong wind tugs at our clothes and hair. The children are excited, whipped up by the elements, wanting to throw stones into the fast-moving water. I am gripped with fear and hold myself back from impulsively pulling the children away from the edge of the river into the opposite direction, away from its wilderness. I keep reminding them to be careful, and the girls laugh 'Mum we won't fall in, so silly', leaving me feeling foolish for my fear but no less fearful. My parents and I would not usually phone each other during the holidays but since my mother had started cancer treatment everything was different. She rang my mobile phone as we were having a packed lunch on the pebbled beach before reaching said river. My mother was unusually tender and celebratory of hearing about our day, where it would usually be tinged with her sadness and my guilt. On that day, I found it hard to receive her love, acutely aware of her impending death.

The willow helped me see that in the place of receiving her love and feeling the pain, I received the wilderness of the river and the fear of it instead. Fear of life, fear of loss, fear of letting go. Sometimes it takes years to receive love and to allow pain.

I continue my walk in the park and the next tree I visit is the yew tree. It's old with multiple trunks fused together, with a cave-like hollow in the middle. I call into the hollow, the sound echoes back to me, and I ask for a message. My matrilineal group speaks to me in one voice, saying "We are here. We are all here waiting for you". I smile and say, "Ok, let's go for a walk". I walk with my mother, her mother Margaret, her mother Ellen, and her mother Brigid, all walking behind me in one line. I see my twin daughters run ahead and disappear. They are busy getting on with life. We enter a woodland, walking along its small pathways that circle around, away from and towards each other, re-joining later by the main path that leads out to a clearing.

I walk over to the Beech tree whose huge branches create a dome. I touch her characteristic smooth bark, lean against her, and ask for guidance. She reminds me that I have learned from her that there is no need to penetrate things when I have questions. That it is ok for that which needs to be known to emerge naturally. No forcing needed. I give thanks and walk on.

I start to think about my great-grandmother Ellen and our shared link of body spasms and the profound sense of 'there is no support', revealed to me all those years ago in the family constellation workshop. Perhaps Ellen has a message for me. I ask Ellen to walk alongside me, and she agrees. Has she got any pearls of wisdom for me? Ellen tells me not to isolate myself from the world. To seek support and help, be part of life and people. I say to her in a young child's voice "but I don't want to". She insists, and says "be brave, and you will see that this will help you". I am struck by Ellen's clarity; her voice has a bell-like quality.

I keep walking pondering on this. What would asking for help look like? My mother comes to mind. I wonder whether I should call my mother to my side. I don't really want to, as this is the kernel of my grief I am pushing away.

I decide to be brave. I call her and she readily comes next to me. She puts her strong arms around me and says "I love you. And I am sorry". I am overcome with emotion, and I say to her "I forgive you. It's hard to be a mother, and to let go, I know this too well. You did what you were able to do". I cry and swear at the tough lessons that being a mother and a daughter throw up in life. I settle down under the branches of an unfamiliar pine tree. The rays of the sun reach me through the clusters of the trees' blue needles. I feel deep sadness thinking about what could have been and at the same time feel embraced by the sun and the tree I am sheltering under.

I continue my walk to the Dawn Redwood. This tree has taught me about vulnerability, to welcome it, to allow softness. I stand by it, touch its bark and lean against its trunk, facing the sun. "Thank you", I say, "you remind me each time with such gentleness not to fear vulnerability. And today the message is clear. *There is no need to fear grief.* Grief is the conduit to change. Leaning into grief is not the end. It's the beginning of something new. Rivers untangled.

The next day I have another osteopathy appointment. The osteopath works on me for quite some time. She tells me that my pelvis has accepted the adjustments she had made the week prior. There wasn't much more she needed to do while she jiggled my legs, gently. To end the treatment, she cups my torso with one hand on my solar plexus and one hand on my spine. To my surprise, my body responds with that ancestral spasm, Ellen and I share. This time I am supported, with gentle hands, and I am grateful that this ancestral tremor is showing up, here, now. The spasms feel like ripples of water over boulders in a strong flowing river. I am letting go. I notice that I am smiling, even though my muscle memory associates this spasm with overwhelm. The osteopath moves onto my left shoulder, cupping the joint with both her hands. My system responds with stillness. My breathing switches into a slow, deep rhythm, and for a flash Bridget's name drops into my mind with the image of a flat, calm sea. I feel touched, as I sense my transition from the river to the sea; held calmly in gentle hands, pain dissolving. Ellen said accept help and find peace, and here it is, showing up through her mother Bridget.

*

A month later I go on a solo trip to the seaside. The choice of location is mostly dependent on ease of travel within the day to be back in time for my son's return from school. I seek out the waterfront, and I am interested in tidal times, excited about the impending change of the landscape that will reveal the sandy beach, that I am eager to touch with my bare feet. But first I walk along the sea path, then up to the hills above. I want to be close to the sky and see the water from above, knowing that their presence will allow my imagination to take flight. Once I finished exploring, I venture as closely as I can to the cliff's edge and lie on my back in the long grass. Looking towards the edge I imagine taking a step off the cliff and into the sky, then step down into the sea. I merge with the elements, the blues and greys of Sky and Water become one, taking me into their fold, whilst resting into Earth.

My merging is a vibration, an aliveness. It is a soaring feeling with a deep-rooted sense of ground.

Suddenly and surprisingly, my grandmother is lying next to me. I wasn't looking for this. An internal voice asks "Granma?" (the voice feels childlike, it's entirely trusting with an unquestionable sense of belonging). Granma affirms her presence. I say hello and she greets me back. After that I just feel her energy. It is round and full. It is warm and comfortable. The intensity of it is such that I can only attune to it for a short while. I then note that I recognize this energy, it makes me think of my daughter who fainted when my mother died. I am astounded. I ask Granma to confirm that they share this energy, and she says yes. We then spend the following few hours together. I'm delighted to find out that she is good company with a mischievous sense of humour. She proclaims that she doesn't like walking much but is more than happy to have fish and chips whilst looking out at sea.

Later, as I walk along the deserted vast coastline, her presence fades. From that day onwards Granma appears as soon as I call her. I say Granma, and she says yes. I tell her about mundane things that happen in my day, and she listens. She is always supportive, always loving. She makes me laugh because she is also grumpy and is not shy to say what she likes and doesn't like. Her love for me and my love for her is an intimate gift I did not expect to receive.

*

A few months later is another Easter, twelve years after my mother's passing. The whole family is reunited, which is nice. As is customary every year since my mother's passing at Easter, there is mention of drama and the fear of it. Over the years I had a fall or two, one of which required stitching, with various other mishaps on Easter Sundays. Last year, my father's sister died unexpectedly on Easter Sunday, which meant I had to re-create that hurried Easter departure to meet death. In short, we had enough dramatic incidences over the years for it to have become an Easter thing to be feared.

What unfolded instead, over several weeks before and after Easter, was more like a re-birth. Chronology and words can't capture several interlacing events that came together to form a whole, the sense of which I can only grasp in retrospect with a feeling that healing had taken place. Granma was present throughout. In the throes of various family members going through both physical and emotional pain, Granma said to me "once this is all over you can get a starfish". What Granma referred to was to add a starfish pendant to the ones I already had acquired to represent each daughter, myself and my mother.

The starfish was a surprising creature that I had no connection to. However, it was a creature of the sea and was a fitting addition to the other pendants that intentionally referenced water or flow.

Indeed, when family matters had settled and the routines had resumed, I did as Granma said and acquired a starfish pendant. To my surprise, once I added the starfish, the five pendants fanned out in a pleasing way, the five tentacles of the starfish creating room for the other pendants to fall into their own place. It felt as though the starfish brought balance into the four generations of our matrilineal group, where each member became visible in their own right.

I've since learned that the starfish lacks a centralized brain and instead relies on a complex nervous system concentrated around its mouth and arms, that guides its decisions for survival.

What if I relied more on my nervous system rather than my thoughts to move into the right direction? The message of the starfish may be about learning to trust the flow instinctively. The right path will reveal itself in good time. In retrospect this matched a message Granma gave me on that day on the hills when she first appeared to me. She said to me "be brave and confident in all things you do".

Relying on my senses is not what I was taught to do and yet my experiences have shown me that incredible things happen when I do.

Connecting to my ancestors and receiving messages from them assisted my personal healing and growth. Each ancestor had a unique quality to how she showed up. Ellen my great-grandmother came with a clarity, her message was about change. She is Water. Granma appeared in a tangible, physical form, transmitting love and belonging, she is Earth. My mother remains largely silent also in her death. It is a mystery that I accept and belongs to Sky. She goes beyond this life on earth. My great-great grandmother

Bridget has been my subtle guide from since my mother died; she is my creative spirit. And my great-great-great grandmother Cecilia may or may not be called for guidance. My relationship to these women is alive and available. As alive and available as the world of trees, plants and creatures. Healing is not just personal but happens at group level. If I feel more whole and settled, then surely, they do to? I've asked my ancestors if this is so, and I am met with cheerful approval.

The flow of moving forward in life, embracing change and growing out of the old into the new is a movement that contains endings, beginnings, endings, beginnings as a continuous stream. The river untangled is the flow, the sea is the containment of and connection to all life.

The journey from the banks of the River Tyne, where four generations of my female ancestors lived, was a journey to the sea of containment and emotional freedom.

The fullness of that journey tells me that I am whole. The flow of the river and the vastness of the sea are telling me

All you need is here, now.

Acknowledgements

Family, friends, and the many supporters of this book, thank you for the conversations and feedback.

Grateful for spaces, people & practices that invite study and reflection; The Open University, Meditation, Art Journalling, Collage, Carl Jung, Sandplay therapy, Donald Winnicott, Existential Phenomenology, Creativity as a life force (MA dissertation), Goldsmiths Library, the Society for Existential Analysis.

Thank you to the world of therapy; my teachers, therapists, peers, supervisors, supervisees, & clients, past and present, a heartfelt thank you to you all.

Thank you to researchers in the field of trauma and body; *The Body keeps the Score*, Bessel van der Kolk, Peter Levine, Bonnie Bainbridge, Donna Eden and Energy Medicine, Energy Psychology and its methods.

Thank you to Shamanic teachings & spirit friends.

A special thank you to my nearest and dearest for your love, support, conversations, stories and inspirations.

About the author

Sara grew up in the German speaking part of Switzerland to migrant parents. She explored different countries and cultures before settling in London, which is now her home. Beside her long-standing psychotherapy practice, she works in the NHS, where she also teaches staff well-being and trauma-informed care. Sara is a mother of three grown up children. Rivers Untangled is her first book.